Recovering
from the Losses
of Life

Recovering from the Losses of Life

H. Norman Wright

Contents

1

The Losses of Life

She stood in front of the large group radiating confidence and assurance. As she interacted with the people, smiling and laughing, it was obvious she was in good spirits. Life seemed to be going well for her.

But several of those in the group she was leading appeared just the opposite. An air of sadness hung over them. A few of them sat stoically. There were no smiles or laughter, no confidence or assurance. After a while, the speaker noticed the ones who seemed to be struggling, and during a break she went over to them.

"I couldn't help noticing that several of you appear sad and are struggling with some problem this evening. Could you tell me what your concerns are?"

One by one, the stories poured out. One man had lost his job after twenty-seven years. A mother had a son who was in the last stages of AIDS. Another woman's husband had been killed three months previously. And one man had chronic undiagnosed back pains.

The speaker listened attentively to the stories of recent upsets and then she said, "I can see we all have something in common.

We're all dealing with significant losses and experiencing a lot of pain.''

A man spoke up. "It's true," he said. *"We* are, but you couldn't be struggling with a major loss. We've watched you this evening, and you are nowhere near where any of us are. You're not struggling as we are."

"You're right," the speaker replied, "when you say that I'm not struggling as you are. I'm not now—but I was. And it was difficult. Two years ago, I was in the same type of situation as many of you: an unfaithful husband, divorce, loss of a home, and my dad died suddenly of a heart attack. I was deep in despair. I am still grieving. I am still recovering from my losses. I'm just at a different step. I was where you are, and someday you will be where I am."

Loss. It's a simple four-letter word that is one of our constant companions throughout life. But we don't talk about it very often. Like a silent conspiracy, we seem to have an unspoken agreement with others not to talk about our losses. Yet with each and every loss comes the potential for change, growth, new insights, understanding, and refinement—all positive descriptions and words of hope. But they are often in the future, and we fail to see that far ahead when we are in the midst of our grief.

Nobody likes to lose. Life is supposed to be filled with winners. Look at the headlines on the sports page. The accolades are given to winners, not losers. Losing hurts. It carries sharpened points that jab into our nerves and cause pain. A small loss or a large one—it doesn't matter. It hurts. And it hurts even more because we have not been taught to expect or how to handle the losses of life. We want to be winners. We want success. We want to be in control of our lives, so we build walls around us with signs that say, "Losses—No Trespassing!" Then, if they occur, we feel violated.

Too often, a person who has suffered a loss is blamed for it: "She must not have been a good wife for him to leave her."

"They failed as parents. Otherwise that child would have stayed in the church and wouldn't have become involved with that crowd."

"He lost his job. I wonder what he did wrong?"

"If they had been living the Christian life, this wouldn't have happened."

Have you ever had such thoughts about another person, or about yourself?

This attitude has been with us for a long time. In John 9, the disciples expressed such thoughts to Jesus about a blind man:

> And as He passed by, He saw a man blind from birth. And His disciples asked Him, saying, "Rabbi, who sinned, this man or his parents, that he should be born blind?" Jesus answered, "It was neither that this man sinned, nor his parents; but it was in order that the works of God might be displayed in him."
>
> John 9:1–3 NAS

You have experienced many losses in your life already. You may not even be aware of some of them, or you may not have realized that what you experienced were actually losses. Some are over in twenty-four hours. Others last for years. How you respond to them or what you let them do to you will affect the rest of your life. You can't avoid loss or shrug it off. Loss is not the enemy; not facing its existence is. Unfortunately, many of us have become more proficient in developing denial than we are in facing and accepting the losses of life.

Even if you attempt to ignore the loss, the emotional experience of it is implanted in your heart and mind, and no eraser will remove it. Whenever there is any kind of an attachment, a loss cannot be avoided when the tie is broken. Life is full of relationships with people, things, and dreams that break up. Then new attachments occur. As each change takes place, you must experience the grief that accompanies it.

The amount or intensity of loss you feel is closely tied to the replaceability of whatever you lost. When you break a favorite piece of sporting equipment or your car burns, your upset will subside in several days or weeks. But the death of a child or a spouse has a different impact. You may decide to have another child or marry again, but you can never replace the original.[1]

Children who experience too many losses have more difficulty handling their future adolescent and adult losses. Children do not have the coping and defense mechanisms that adults have. They don't possess the verbal skills or the creative fantasy to generate alternatives that adults possess.

Some children become so sensitized to the pain of loss that in later years their losses are felt so deeply, there is a predisposition to depression. I have seen many adults who experienced some form of loss as children that created an oversensitivity to similar reactions and responses as adults. One forty-year-old man lived in a conditional-love atmosphere as he was growing up. Whenever he was noisy or disruptive, love and acceptance were pulled away from him. He felt empty and hurt each time he experienced this loss of love. It was so bad that when his friends came over to see him, he would become embarrassed if they were loud or noisy in front of his parents. Today, he is very sensitive to the responses of others in noisy situations, even when he isn't responsible for the noise.

Rejection is a very difficult loss for children to handle. Dr. Hugh Missildine describes the effects of it:

> It is difficult to feel at home in the world if you have never felt at home in your own home. If you were rejected as a child, you have an extreme emotional handicap; you are, in effect, the original person "without a country."
>
> You may see yourself as an outlaw, unacceptable to your-

self and to others. Your self-depreciation is bitter and you
feel, almost automatically, bitterness toward others that
leads you often to distort the attitudes of others.[2]

Unfortunately, most adults are unable to help their children
grieve because they have never learned to properly grieve themselves. When a child doesn't grieve over a loss, a similar loss in
adult life can reactivate the feelings associated with the childhood
experience. Thus a childhood loss can predispose us to oversensitivity and then depression.

Several years ago, a woman at a Crisis Counseling seminar
shared an experience with me. She and her husband had moved
to a new city three years before. Prior to that time, they had lived
in the same town for fifteen years. They were deeply involved in
their church and had a large number of friends. Their children
had been raised there, and they had celebrated each Christmas
with the same close family friends.

When they moved, they left all of that behind. The woman's
husband started his new job immediately. However, because of
the nature of her profession, she had to start over again and
rebuild from scratch. For the first two years, she experienced a
significant amount of depression and couldn't figure out why.
Finally she went for counseling, and as she focused on her family
of origin, the reason became apparent. As a child, up to the age
of five, she bonded more with her grandmother than with her
mother. They were very close, but then her grandmother died
suddenly. Within weeks, her family moved from town to the
country, where the nearest neighbor was a mile away. As she and
her therapist talked and the connection became clear, she then
was able to grieve as she never had over her grandmother and that
childhood move. In time, her depression lifted.

Was there a loss in your life you have never really grieved
over? You may want to reflect on that question for a while.

Too many early-childhood losses can predispose us to oversensitivity and depression by teaching us to "compound" our losses. Compounding is a way of responding in which we begin to pile one loss on top of another. Instead of experiencing one loss at a time and focusing the grief on that loss, compounding creates a bigger loss. Consequently, each loss appears to be larger than it actually is. It is important to isolate each loss, see it for what it is, respond to it, and then deal with the other losses individually. It is fairly common to compound our losses, but when that happens, we must unpack them, separate them, and focus our thinking on them one by one.[3]

Life is a blending of loss and gain, loss and acquisition. In creation, loss is the ingredient of growth. A bud is lost when it turns into a beautiful rose. When a plant pushes its way up through the soil, a seed is lost.

When you were a child, your baby teeth came in after bouts of pain and crying. But one day, they began to loosen and wiggle and soon fell out or were pulled. They were lost to make room for the permanent teeth. Sometimes these too are lost and replaced by false teeth.

Graduating from high school produced a loss of status, friends, and familiarity, but most of us looked forward to it, for it meant going on with our lives. When we are young, some of our losses are celebrated as much as they are mourned. Most of these early losses are developmental and quite necessary. We can accept them fairly easily. But often we focus on the gain without remembering that there is usually some loss attached to it. Change involves some form of loss of the way things were at one time.

Any event that destroys a person's understanding of the meaning of life is felt as a loss. Our beliefs and expectations come under attack. The phrase, "How could they have done such a thing?" expresses this confusion.

More and more immigrants are coming to our country, both legally and illegally. These immigrants experience a major cultural loss of life-style. Gone are the normal and familiar elements that give life meaning, such as road signs, money, language, familiar faces, role patterns, food, and relationships.

Missionaries who move to new fields to minister face major adjustments and losses. Every four years they return to their homeland to encounter new losses as they confront the rapid changes of our own economy, values, and life-style.

Economic losses abound today. We may not even realize that an increase at the gas pumps or inflation is a loss to each one of us.

There are other more subtle losses that affect us. We may be aware of the pain of an experience, but we don't identify it as a loss. A minor failure or "putting your foot in your mouth" socially can create embarrassment, shame, or disappointment. The expression "loss of face" recognizes the "lost" characteristic of these experiences.

Losses can be obvious: losing loved ones through death or divorce, a car is stolen, a house is vandalized and robbed. Other losses may not be so obvious: changing jobs, receiving a *B* instead of an *A* in a college course, getting less than we had hoped for in a raise, moving, illness (loss of health), a new teacher in the middle of a semester, the change from an office with windows to one without, success or achievement (the loss of striving or challenge or even relationships with fellow workers), a son or daughter going off to school, the loss of an ideal, a dream, or a lifelong goal. All of these are losses, but because they may not be easy to recognize, we do not identify them as such. Therefore, we do not spend time and energy dealing with them.

Many of the losses in life are related to aging. As we grow older, the dreams and beliefs of childhood begin to crumble and change. Remember the first crush you had on the opposite sex? All childhood and adolescent romances are filled with losses, some daily, even hourly! Moving on from school to school, failing a grade, dropping out, leaving home for college, or just moving out—even if the change was planned for, an element of loss is involved.

When you hit the job market, losses multiply as rejections occur. Someone else gets the raise or promotion, deals fall through, court cases are lost, businesses fail, the economy falters, you get stuck in a "going nowhere" job.

Then come the physical losses—ironically, a major one involves the gain of pounds and inches! We lose our youth, our beauty, our smooth skin, our muscle tone, our shape, our hair, our vision and hearing, our sexual ability or interest, and so on.

In the middle years, the losses take on a different flavor. Now they seem to be more frequent, permanent, and in many cases, negative. Who rejoices over losing hair, teeth, or graduating to bifocals or even trifocals? We don't usually call these "growth experiences." It seems that losses now seem to build on other losses.[4]

Consider also the frequency of losses. We don't usually lose many of our friends through death early in life. But in our later years, it becomes much more frequent. The longer we live, the more losses of friends and relatives we experience.

When you are younger, you may have one physical problem, and it is corrected. But now, these problems accumulate. Muscles don't work as well or recover as fast. You're slower in your response time and one day you notice that, in addition to the new glasses, people are talking in softer tones and you even have to adjust the television volume higher!

We seem to handle losses best when they are infrequent. But after mid-life, we move into a time zone of accumulated losses. It is difficult to handle the next one when we are still recovering from the present one. Our coping skills may be overtaxed, and if they were never highly developed, these losses are going to hit us quite hard.

The other difficulty with losses is their finality. If you lose a job at age twenty-seven, you simply look around for another. But what if you lose your job of thirty years at age fifty-seven? What do you do now, especially if this is all you know how to do, and there isn't as much demand for your skills anymore?

Losing a spouse when you are older is limiting as well. If you divorce or your partner dies when you are young, it is much easier to find another mate. As you get older, it becomes more difficult, especially if you are a woman. Most women who are over fifty and lose their husbands do not remarry.[5]

In his book *Losses in Later Life,* R. Scott Sullender shows how handicapped people can teach us to turn life's losses into triumphs:

> There is a handicapped person in your future: you! Handicapped persons are dealing in the present moment with what you and I will have to deal with later. Sooner or later each of us will become handicapped in one way or another. Sooner or later each of us will have to deal with one or several major losses in our health. Then we will travel down the same path that the handicapped person currently walks. Then we will know their pain, frustration and sufferings. Perhaps if we could learn from them now, whatever our age, we would be better prepared for our own future.
>
> Handicapped persons teach us that life is more than a body. They demonstrate the truth of all of the great religions that the things that make us truly human and truly divine are not physical qualities. They are qualities of the Spirit. St. Paul listed a few of these qualities: love, joy, peace, patience, kindness, goodness, faithfulness, gentleness, self-control (Galatians 5:22). Jesus listed a few more: meekness, peacemaking, purity of heart, mercy, hunger for righteousness, suffering in a right cause (Matthew 5:3–10). Neither of them mentioned physical beauty or even physical health. The qualities that save us do not include the shape of our bodies.

Handicapped persons also can teach us how to suffer and how to rise above bodily limitations. Sometimes pain cannot be fixed, nor can all limitations be conquered. Most of us will have to deal with pain and limitations, at first in minor ways and later in major ways. We will learn new meanings for the word ''courage.'' Either we will rise above our limitations and learn to live with them or we shall sink to new lows of despair, bitterness and helplessness. The choice depends largely on the strength of our courage.

In a sense, then, a handicap or a loss of health can become a gift. It never starts out that way. Initially it is a horrible loss. If through the loss, however, we can learn to nurture our spiritual qualities and learn the art of suffering well, then we will have transformed our loss into a gain. We will have grown in and through our loss. We will have risen above our loss precisely by not letting it defeat us, but by letting it propel us forward into a more advanced stage of human existence. Admittedly, not everyone makes such a major leap forward. Neither have some human beings made it past a Sunday school theology. Yet, the loss of health in later life, as horrible as it seems, can be the opportunity for growing toward an ever greater level of spiritual maturity.[6]

Identity losses may occur periodically throughout our lifetime. These are difficult for many people because of the intangibility of the issues. But they are real and they have the potential for either destruction or tremendous growth. These will be discussed in detail in a later chapter.

The most difficult losses of life are the threatened losses. The possibility of their occurring is real, but there is little you can do about it. Your sense of control is destroyed. You have been working for nineteen years at the same company. At twenty years, all of your benefits are secure. Then you are informed that, due to a sluggish economy and lost contracts, 40 percent of the employees at your company will be terminated at the end of the month, and length of employment is no criteria for being retained. Will you be one of the 40 percent?

There are many other threatened losses in life . . .

. . . waiting the outcome of a biopsy.

. . . a spouse saying, "I'm thinking of divorcing you."

. . . a romantic interest who doesn't call you regularly anymore.

. . . a business investment that may not come through.

. . . being sued by an angry employee or customer.

. . . being in a foreign country and the government threatens to retain everyone as hostages.

. . . a friend tells you he suspects your son has been using drugs for the past year.

All of the above are potential losses. They could occur. There is little you can do about them, and you feel the loss before it occurs—you feel helpless.

Even the delight of having a child brings accompanying losses. As one young mother put it, "I never realized all the adjustments having a baby would bring. My time is not my own, my energy is gone, my body is not my own, our intimacy and romance has been shelved, and I feel like a prisoner at home. I can't go out when I want to anymore. I feel as if I've lost out in life!"

These adjustments or losses are quite common. They can be anticipated and even planned for to ease their impact. But the majority of losses we experience are difficult to grieve over. Why? Because they are not usually recognized as losses.

> The trouble with trying to mourn loss when death isn't involved is that there is no body, no funeral, and no public shoulder to cry on. There is no traditional, socially sanctioned outlet for mourning when the loss isn't death.
>
> Loss of function, relationship, or financial resources, for example, bring no printed obituary, no "remains" laid to

rest, no public gathering to cement the fact and focus love
on the mourner.

Trying to mourn loss when death is not involved is a
lonely hell, with vague beginnings and endings defined
more often by the intangible dimensions of lost and found
hope than by the perimeters of the crisis itself.[7]

We all live with fear, some more than others. The fear of loss
is deeply ingrained within all of us. Every loss we experience
from early infancy on becomes part of this pool of fear within us.
Sometimes people wear items or amulets around their necks as
protection against misfortune, which is another way of saying
loss. We are afraid of misfortune, and we tend to avoid those who
have experienced it for fear it might be contagious.

Whenever a loss occurs, it is important to see it in the context
of your life experiences so you understand the full impact of what
has happened. Identifying all of the accompanying losses as well
as the impact of this loss on your thinking toward future events is
important. Remember that past losses have an effect on current
losses and attachments, and all of these factors affect your fear of
future loss and your ability to make future attachments.

During the experience of loss, there may be hidden questions
that need to be addressed at some point:

Will I recover from this loss? Will I survive?

Is it all right to continue with my life without whatever or
whomever has been lost to me?

Can I be happy and fulfilled knowing that the person I've lost
is really gone and my life will now be different?[8] In succeeding
chapters we will attempt to answer some of these questions.

Notes

Chapter 1 The Losses of Life

1. Dr. Ronald W. Ramsay and Rene Noorbergen, *Living With Loss*
   (New York: William Morrow and Co. Inc., 1981), 47, 48, adapted.

2. W. Hugh Missildine, *Your Inner Child of the Past* (New York: Simon & Schuster, Inc., 1968), 59.

3. Archibald Hart, *Counseling the Depressed* (Waco, Texas: Word Books, 1987), 123–127, adapted.

4. R. Scott Sullender, *Losses in Later Life* (New York: Paulist Press, 1989), 3, adapted.

5. Ibid., 16–18, adapted.

6. Ibid., 142, 143.

7. Nina Hermann Donnelly, *I Never Know What to Say* (New York: Ballantine Books, 1987), 123.

8. Bob Deits, *Life After Loss* (Tucson: Fisher Books, 1988), 37, adapted.

2

Losses We Never Considered

Think for a moment about the losses you have experienced and how they have impacted you. What were the three or four most difficult times of your life? What losses were involved? Were they obvious or subtle? Did you recognize them as losses at that time?

It is vital that you identify every loss in your life for what it is—a loss—and then grieve for it, just as you would for someone who died. For several years, I have been asking my counselees the question, "What losses have you experienced that you never fully grieved for?" Most of them, either immediately or within two or three weeks, are able to recognize some issue they had previously failed to see as a loss and therefore had failed to grieve for. When we don't grieve properly, unresolved reactions and feelings lead to a higher level of discomfort, and these unresolved issues continue to prevent us from living life to the fullest.

It is also important to discover the "secondary losses" that are results of the initial loss. These can be actual visible losses or subtle changes involving our relationships with others, status, environment, living style, hopes, dreams, wishes, and fantasies.

One of my students lost his older brother in a traffic accident. This older brother had been responsible for the care of their elderly parents. But now he was gone, and this student felt that he should take over the care of his parents. This caused him to drop out of school, delay his education, change vocational direction, postpone additions to his own family, and limit his time with his wife, child, friends, and hobbies. Do you see all the secondary losses involved?

Entire groups can experience a loss. When a highly loved minister leaves his congregation after fifteen years, the whole congregation experiences grief and all the accompanying stages. Unfortunately, it can make things difficult for the new minister following in his footsteps.

There is a loss associated with the anticipation of an achievement that never comes to fruition. You've seen it on television: at the end of a major sports event, athletes hang their heads in sorrow or weep silently when they lose a game. Politicians cry before the cameras following defeat in an election. They not only lost the election but there is also a loss of pride, a loss of anticipated income, and a loss of self-worth. All these were anticipated losses. The contenders never really had what they lost, but it doesn't make their grief any less real.

The loss of an ideal creates a powerful type of grief. Where were you on November 22, 1963, when the news came over the airwaves that President Kennedy had been shot and killed? The entire country entered into a collective mourning process. Jackie's grief was not just her grief but ours as well. When Kennedy died, we lost a dream and an ideal as well as a man.

How many times in your life have you changed residences? Years ago, my family and I moved four times in three years. Each year forty million people move to new locations. Alvin Toffler gave a label to these frequent travelers. He called them "the mournful movers" in his book *Future Shock*. A move like this involves more than moving. It includes the loss of the familiar, the routine, friends, church, shopping mall, doctors, schools. But a move is not usually given the recognition it needs as a major loss in our lives.[1]

The loss of a portion of the body or a bodily function is becoming much more frequent as longevity increases. At the present time there are over thirty-five thousand limb amputations annually in our country, as well as a large number of mastectomies and hysterectomies.

Having a disease such as cancer is considered a major loss because of the health change. But have you considered all of the additional secondary losses? Some are physical and some symbolic. There is the loss of a familiar home environment because of the stay in a hospital room. There is the loss of independence because of the illness and having to rely upon others for care. There is a loss of control for patients confined to bed.

But these are not all of the losses involved. A disease such as cancer has a devastating and often numbing effect upon its victims. A cancer patient may experience a loss of autonomy, loss of bodily functions, loss of body parts, loss of predictability, loss of pleasure, loss of identity, loss of intimacy, loss of hope, loss of job, loss of enjoyable hobbies, loss of social interaction or contacts, loss of self-esteem, and possible loss of mobility.

Every lesser loss that is experienced compounds the overall feeling of loss a person experiences. And each loss needs a grief reaction! Each one needs to be mourned. The meaning and extent of each loss varies for each person, depending upon the investment that was made; thus the amount of grieving required varies.

When a loss is permanent, it brings with it the sense that something has really ended. It is true that we might try to resist or avoid the reality, but when something is final we do have to make a new life without its existence.

When a loss is temporary or seems to be, you have a situation in which there is no closure. Thus there is a recurring sense of loss. In the case of servicemen missing in action or runaway children, a reunion may frequently be imagined, alternating with the fearful thought, *He may never return.* The constant fantasies of regaining what appears to be lost add to the intensity of the loss.[2]

A person with cancer who has always been concerned with how he or she looks will be greatly impacted by the loss of a body part. Another person may be most affected by the change in work and recreational involvements, whereas someone else would be more affected by the limited social contacts.

Most people, however, don't identify their losses separately. They don't break them down and grieve for each one. Unfortunately, this makes the grief more intense, and the recovery process and new attachments are delayed.[3]

The death of a significant person is a major loss, but you have to identify all of the secondary losses as well. That can include the loss of hopes, dreams, wishes, fantasies, feelings, expectations, and the needs you had for that person. It is not only what you lose in the present but in the future as well. A widow has not only lost her husband but has also lost a partner to share retirement, church functions, couples groups, a child's wedding, a grandchild's first birthday, and so on. Perhaps you have lost a significant person during the past few months or years. Are you aware of the extent of this loss?

Identifying some of the roles that a deceased person played in your life may help you understand the direction your life will now be taking. Think of someone close you have lost, or think about what it would be like if the person died. Circle any of the following that apply and then list additional roles not mentioned here:

friend	parent
handyperson	brother
lover	sister
gardener	provider
companion	cook
sports partner	bill payer
checkbook balancer	laundry person
mechanic	confidant(e)
encourager	mentor
motivator	prayer partner
business partner	source of inspiration or insight
errand person	teacher
tax preparer	counselor
spouse	protector
child	organizer

Now is it clearer?

Seven months before I started writing this book, I experienced one of the major losses of my life. My son Matthew died. He was twenty-two years old and was profoundly mentally retarded. All through his life we experienced losses. The dreams and hopes I had for a son were lost. Even being able to hear him call me "Daddy" wasn't a reality, except for once or twice. Seeing expressions of joy and delight at times that called for these emotions was nonexistent. The personal fulfillment of selecting a Christmas and birthday gift for him each year was lost, for there was very little that he would respond to or that he would use. We gradually got used to these losses and accepted them. But when Matthew died, an entirely new set of losses was introduced to our lives.

We could no longer look through the catalogs to select his special sleepwear; nor could we stop by Salem Christian Home (where he lived for the past eleven years) to take him out to lunch. There is the future loss of not having Matthew home on Thanksgiving or Christmas or taking him to Knott's Berry Farm on his birthday. And there are little additional unanticipated losses that occur weekly. We don't call the home anymore to see how he's doing, a subject of conversation is gone, and certain phrases or expressions we would say to him are no longer said. My wife and I must face and grieve over each loss in order to move on with our lives.

The losses of our adult life may be compounded by the remaining unresolved losses of our childhood. We bring these into our adult life like unwelcome excess baggage. The losses vary in their complexity and their intensity. Some children are never allowed or encouraged to grieve over the loss of their favorite pet. They are told, ''Don't cry. It's just a cat,'' or ''We'll get you a new one tomorrow.''

Sometimes it is a case of unexplained withdrawal of involvement on the part of the parents. When John was a child, both of his parents were actively involved with him in all of his soccer, little league, and school activities. But when he turned eleven, with no explanation, they not only stopped attending his activities but they didn't even ask him about them. He couldn't understand it and ached inside for some response on their part. But it never came. This disappointment led to a fear that ''everyone will end up doing this to me,'' and consequently a sense of caution and suspicion began to develop.

More and more adults come into adulthood with a sense of loss because they were children of divorce. Several years ago, *Newsweek* magazine estimated that 45 percent of all children will live with only one parent at some time before they are eighteen years old. The results of studies on children of divorce indicate that the effects of divorce on children are more serious and long lasting than many divorced parents are willing to admit. Studies released in England in 1978 showed that children of divorce have a shorter life expectancy and more illness than children in families in which no divorce occurred. These children tend to leave school sooner as well. In New York City, which has a very high adolescent suicide

rate, two out of every three teenage suicides occur among teen-
agers whose parents are divorced. Many others carry a pattern of
insecurity, depression, anxiety, and anger into their adult years
because of the extent of the losses they experienced.

In divorce, children experience many types of losses. These
not only include the disruption of the family unit but also the
possible permanent loss of one of the parents, the loss of a home,
neighborhood, school friends, standard of living, family outings,
family holiday get-togethers, self-esteem, and so on.

When a parent dies, there is a sense of closure to the relationship and an opportunity to say a final good-bye. The child goes
through a rather predictable period and sequence of mourning.
But where is the mourning period after a divorce? It is open-
ended. It comes and goes, depending upon the involvement of the
noncustodial parent. If the parent does not stay involved, a child
feels, *Is Mom [Dad] ever coming back? If not, why not? What did
I do?* The child doesn't know whether the loss will be permanent
or temporary. The occasional birthday card, the weekly phone
call, and the all-too-infrequent visits and vacations keep the fantasy that the parent might return alive. (For additional information on this, *see* my book *Always Daddy's Girl* and *Divorced
Kids* by Laurene Johnson and Georglyn Rosenfeld.)

We are hearing more and more about physical and sexual
abuse of children. This is a damaging loss that contaminates
adulthood. It is demeaning, takes away the innocence of children, and violates their perception of adults. They often learn to
suffer silently. They have lost the love of a parent, their dreams,
and their innocence. They have lost out on their childhood!

Another damaging loss is abandonment. It is true that some
children are physically abandoned, but this number is far sur-
passed by those who have been emotionally abandoned. Often
children cannot understand why they feel so alone and abandoned. They know their parents never leave them alone and their
physical needs are met, but their emotional needs are neglected.

There is no nurturing, hugging, or emotional intimacy. The verbal affirmations children so desperately need are shrouded in silence. Soon they begin to wonder, *What is wrong with me?* This perception is carried with them throughout their adult lives.

Time and time again I have seen the ungrieved-for losses of childhood interfere with an adult's way of responding to life and marriage. The type and number of losses a child experiences are too many to identify here. Our main concerns are, *What can be done about those damaging losses of childhood? Is recovery available?* The answer to both questions is a definite yes! It involves relinquishing a perspective that may have been with us for years. But it is possible to recover from those losses of childhood.

There are times when we lose hope and remain stuck with pain from the past. Have you ever caught some flies and imprisoned them in a glass jar with air holes at the top? Some of us did this as children. If you do this, you will notice that the flies buzz around frantically looking for a way out of the jar. But keep the jar closed for several days and something interesting begins to happen. When you take the perforated lid off, the flies don't try to escape. Even though there is no lid, the flies are so used to flying around in a circle, they continue to do so. And even when they get close to the top, they go right back to flying around in a circle. Well, sometimes people do the same thing. We carry our losses with us like emotional baggage, and even though the lid of the jar has been removed, we continue to fly in circles.

When the losses of childhood are identified and confronted, the process of letting them go is anything but passive. It is a very active endeavor. Time will not heal those wounds because the memory has such a foothold. It will take all the steps of grieving, letting go, and saying good-bye that are found in the remaining chapters of this book. There is an abundance of books available on the issue of being free from the past that can also be used. Some of these are my book *Making Peace With Your Past, Cut-*

ting Loose by Howard Halpern, *Adult Children of Legal and Emotional Divorce* by Jim Conway, and *Love Is a Choice* by Minirth-Meier.

When a child is wounded by losses in childhood, he or she could develop a tendency toward depression. For some there is a prevailing sense of sadness that lingers just beneath the surface. Occasional journeys into this realm are normal and give depth and balance to our lives. Sadness can cause us to become more contemplative, serious, thoughtful, and grateful and can give us a new purpose for living life to the fullest. However, constant sadness takes the sunshine and delight out of life.

I remember a day when the sadness of a continual loss hit me again. At the time, our retarded son was seventeen years old. A friend and I met for an early-morning racquetball game. He shared with me that he had taken his six-year-old son on an overnight camping trip. They slept in a tent, made their breakfast over a fire, and played together in the stream. As he went into detail, sharing his excitement and delight, part of me was happy with him, but another part was very uncomfortable. I even wished he would stop telling me about the trip.

I soon realized what was happening: I was once again feeling a sense of loss. I wished I had been able to have those experiences with my son, but I never would. The time was past, never to be retrieved. Matthew's limited capabilities would not allow this experience to be one he and I would ever share together. I felt the loss once more, and a sense of sadness was with me for the entire day. But it was an experience that God used when I shared it with a client to help him begin to feel and live. I also shared this with Joyce, my wife, and it was a time of our drawing closer together. The sadness lifted the next day, and I had changed because of that brief experience. It is now another one of the memories that make up my past but gives a deeper meaning and depth to life. I could handle the loss because I was an adult and understood the complexity of losses, grief, and God's compassion and comfort. Not so with children who experience loss repeatedly. Their abilities are limited, and they become very susceptible to recurring hurt, sadness, and depression.

Think about your life as a child. Have you identified the losses? Do they loom out of proportion to all of your experiences and affect the way you perceive all of your life? This often happens. We all perceive life from our backlog of experiences because our memories are always with us. Our perceptions happen automatically, and we believe that what we perceive is actually the real world.

The way we perceive is similar to a camera. Photographers can alter the image of reality through the use of various lenses or filters. Thus what the camera records may not be an accurate view of the world. A wide-angle lens gives a much wider panorama, but the objects in the picture appear more distant and smaller. A telephoto lens has a much narrower and more selective view of life. It can focus on a beautiful flower, but at the same time it shuts out the rest of the garden. A normal lens will capture happy and smiling people, but those same people seen through a fish-eye lens become distorted and unreal. Filters can blur reality, break images into pieces, bring darkness into a lighted scene, and even create a mist.

Like the lenses and filters on a camera, our perception of the world can become distorted. Depression focuses upon the darker portions of life and takes away the warmth and joy from a scene. A photographer is aware of the distortion in his perception of reality. When we are depressed, we are practically blind without knowing it. The greater the intensity of our depression, the greater the distortion. All this can happen because of overwhelming losses as children.[4]

Who taught you how to handle the losses of life? Probably no one, not even your church. In our families, we are taught that acquisition, whether of material or nonmaterial things, is the way to be happy and satisfied.

We learn to be good in order to acquire attention and praise from parents and other adults. In school, the acquisition of grades gives acceptance and approval. Parents rarely teach us how to handle loss, disappointment, and failure.

The drive to acquire continues throughout life. Isn't this what the advertisers tell us is needed to be successful? Thus we grow up with the myth that "acquiring is normal. Loss is abnormal." Loss to us feels wrong and unnatural.

What are the losses you expect to experience in the next five to ten years? How you respond to losses today and tomorrow may be the result of how you respond to the early losses in your life.

Use the following questions to help you recognize how your past losses are influencing your life today:

1. Reflect on one of the earliest significant losses in your life. When did it happen? How old were you? Where was it? Who were the people involved? What actually happened?
2. What were your feelings at the time?
3. What were your reactions to the loss? Which were positive? Which were negative?
4. Did anyone give you suggestions or advice on how to handle the loss?
5. What did you learn about loss as a result of your early experience? Can you remember any statements that have stayed with you through the years?
6. What did you learn then that may be *hindering* the way you cope with loss today?
7. What did you learn about loss at an early age that *helps* you today?

Now think of the most recent loss you have experienced:

1. Identify the specific loss. Where? What? Who? When?
2. What were your feelings at the time?
3. What were your reactions to the loss? Which were positive? Which were negative?

4. Did anyone give you suggestions or advice on how to handle the loss?
5. What did you learn about loss as a result of your experience? How did others suggest you handle it?
6. How did your early experiences with loss affect the way you responded to this loss?
7. List three healthy things you will do to respond to the next loss you encounter.

Every loss is important. It is part of life and cannot be avoided. Losses are necessary! You grow by losing and then accepting the loss. Change occurs through loss. Growth occurs through loss. Life takes on a deeper and richer meaning because of losses. The better you handle them, the healthier you will be and the more you will grow. No one said that loss was fair, but it is part of life.

For example, lobsters experience a major loss each year. They shed their protective shells, making them vulnerable to the attack of other sea creatures. What a terrible risk! But there are two purposes for this loss and period of risk: the mating process occurs, and there is a growth spurt. Without this, the species would remain stunted and eventually die out.

Perhaps loss traumatizes us so much because it carries with it the message, "You really are not in charge of your life. You don't have much control over your destiny. You are at the mercy of whatever happens."

We all like to be in control of our lives—or at least we like to think we are. Loss of control is one of our most common fears. The things we value most are the very things we feel we must have control over: power, prestige, a person, a job, status, an object, a situation, and so on. You can take charge of some losses; you can create and orchestrate them. A man who quits his job feels he retains some control over his career, even though the aspect of loss is still present. But if he is fired, the loss is greater because he has lost control. A woman who chooses a job transfer to a new city feels she still has control over her situation. But if she is told to transfer or lose her job, she feels out of control. The intensity of the loss is greater.

Some people take control in their lives because they fear the control, influence, or direction of others. Controlling behavior is the fear of trusting others. It's the fear of not being in charge of your own destiny or direction in life. It's the feeling that boasts, "I know what's best for me. I have all the knowledge and skill necessary to direct my life."

People with rigid personalities, such as highly dominant, controlling people or perfectionists, have difficulty handling loss because they do not have much flexibility. Instead of being resilient, they are brittle. The more unexpected the loss, the more trouble they have. Setbacks cause them to make adjustments and changes, and this causes them difficulty. In addition to their rigidity, they lack a wide range of coping skills, and this exacerbates the problem. Consider the fallacy and futility of being in rigid control through the words of Dr. Lloyd John Ogilvie:

> I wonder how controllers like these get along with God. I wonder how they learn to trust Jesus Christ as Savior. I wonder how they try to determine God's will for their lives (or maybe that question never enters their minds). I wonder how controllers handle the unexpected and uncontrollable losses of life and learn to view these upsets with a spiritual perspective. A controller cannot trust God because he fears the control of his life resting in anyone's hands but his own.

On the issue of control and fear as it relates to spiritual life, Ogilvie states:

> Our need to be in charge of ourselves, others, and situations often makes our relationship with Christ life's biggest

power struggle. We are reluctant to relinquish our control and allow Him to run our lives. We may believe in Him and be active in the church and Christian causes, but trusting Him as Lord of everything in life can be scary. Even though we pray about our challenges and problems, all too often what we really want is strength to accomplish what we've already decided is best for ourselves and others.

Meanwhile, we press on with our own priorities and plans. We remain the scriptwriter, casting director, choreographer, and producer of the drama of our own lives, in which we are the star performer.[5]

Can you relate to any of the above? Do you identify with any part of it?

It is true that trusting another person—even God—is risky. Living by faith may be a new experience for you. But living a life of faith in Jesus Christ is far less risky than living a life of faith in yourself. Trying to control your life imprisons you in the need to be in control. Trusting in His control leads to a life of freedom rather than a life of bondage.

What we all need to remember is this: We never *were* in total control! We are not in total control now! We never will be in total control! God, not us, is in control. Why stay in bondage to the myth that we must be in control? There is a better way to live.

I wonder what would happen to us if we placed the control of our lives in Christ's hands for thirty days? It just might help us better handle the losses of life.

I know this is a strange question, but have you ever considered the benefits that accompany loss? For Christians, the issue of loss does have an additional meaning: spiritual growth. It is not automatic and there are many who regress spiritually when confronted with loss. But it is an opportunity to "grow into the likeness of Christ."

Loss can strengthen our faith. It enables us to trust more in God and His resources than in ourselves. With every loss, we are

reminded of the fact that we are not in control and we are not
self-sufficient. Every loss allows us to rest in the grace of God.
Loss enables us to change our perspective and allows our hope
and anticipation of the life to come to grow (2 Corinthians 4:17
ff.). Paul was directed by God to proclaim the message to us that
we can rejoice or exult in our tribulations or sufferings (Romans 5:3).

Loss produces maturity. There are character qualities such as
patience, endurance, humility, long-suffering, gratitude, and self-
control that can develop through our losses:

> Moreover—let us also be full of joy now! Let us exult
> and triumph in our troubles and rejoice in our sufferings,
> knowing that pressure and affliction and hardship produce
> patient and unswerving endurance. And endurance (forti-
> tude) develops maturity of character—that is, approved
> faith and tried integrity. And character of this sort pro-
> duces the habit of joyful and confident hope of eternal sal-
> vation.
>
> Romans 5:3, 4 AMPLIFIED

We live in a world that demands immediate satisfaction.
Losses teach us the lesson that it doesn't always work that way.
We cannot have what we want, when we want it, no matter
what.

When you experience a loss, like Paul your beliefs can change.
Paul discovered the purpose of losses. In 2 Corinthians 12:1–10
he talked about his thorn in the flesh. He wanted it to leave and
it wouldn't. But he learned that there was a purpose for this
"thorn." God's power would be more evident in His life because
of its presence.

When you experience loss, you will discover the extent of the
comfort of God:

Blessed be the God and Father of our Lord Jesus Christ, the Father of sympathy and the God of every consolation and comfort and encouragement; Who consoles and comforts and encourages us in every trouble so that we may also be able to console those who are in any kind of trouble or distress, with the consolation with which we ourselves are consoled and comforted and encouraged by God.

For just as Christ's sufferings fall to our lot as they overflow upon His disciples, and we share and experience them abundantly, so through Christ comfort and consolation and encouragement are also shared and experienced abundantly by us. But if we are troubled, it is for your comfort and for your salvation; and if we are comforted, it is for your comfort and consolation and encouragement, which work in you when you patiently endure the same evils that we also suffer and undergo. And our hope for you—that is, our joyful and confident expectation of good for you—is ever unwavering, assured and unshaken; for we know that just as you share and are partners in our sufferings and calamities, you also share and are partners in our comfort. For we do not want you to be uninformed, brethren, about the affliction and oppressing distress which befell us in the province of Asia, how we were so utterly and unbearably weighed down and crushed that we despaired even of life itself.

Indeed, we felt within ourselves that we had received the sentence of death; but that was to keep us from trusting and depending on ourselves instead of on God Who raises the dead.

For it is He Who rescued and saved us from such a perilous death, and He will still rescue and save us; in and on Him we have set our hope that He will again deliver us from danger and destruction and draw us to Himself, While you also co-operate by your prayers for us—helping and laboring together with us. Thus the lips of

many persons Godward turned will give thanks on our be-
half for the grace granted us at the request of the many
who have prayed.

                              2 Corinthians 1:3–11 AMPLIFIED

God is involved in our lives and reaches out to sustain us. Loss
can bring people together in a way never experienced before. Our
pain creates a deeper sense of empathy and concern for the pain
of others. I have discovered this over the years, especially with
both the parents of handicapped people and the handicapped
themselves. There is a spontaneous response of compassion and
desire to assist whenever I meet someone in that situation. We are
a people who have been called to comfort one another (1 Thes-
salonians 4:18) and to weep with those who weep (Romans
12:15).

Our losses are going to change our values. The questions,
"Why did I spend so much time on that?" and "Why did I waste
all those years?" are common when one is grieving over the loss
of a loved one. Hopefully we learn through those experiences to
the extent that our lives are different.[6]

Our grief work is not really complete until we have found some
meaning in our grief. It is true that our emotions need healing,
but so does our belief system or theology. This is a new thought
to many people.

Notes

Chapter 2 Losses We Never Considered

1. R. Scott Sullender, *Grief and Growth* (New York: Paulist Press,
   1985), 11–16, adapted.

2. Kenneth R. Mitchell and Herbert Anderson, *All Our Losses, All Our
   Griefs* (Philadelphia: The Westminster Press, 1983), 48, adapted.

3. Therese A. Rando, *Grieving: How to Go On Living When Someone You Love Dies* (Lexington, Massachusetts: Lexington Books, 1988), 15, 16, adapted.

4. Richard F. Berg and Christine McCartney, *Depression and the Integrated Life* (New York: Alba House, 1981), 34, adapted.

5. Lloyd John Ogilvie, *Twelve Steps to Living Without Fear* (Dallas, Texas: WORD Incorporated, 1987), 133.

6. Sullender, *Grief and Growth*, 96–101, adapted.

3
The Meaning of Grief

When you enter into grief, you enter into the valley of shadows. There is nothing heroic or noble about grief. It is painful. It is work. It is a lingering process. But it is necessary for all kinds of loss. It has been labeled everything from intense mental anguish to acute sorrow to deep remorse.

There are a multitude of emotions involved in the grief process that seem out of control and often appear in conflict with one another. With each loss comes bitterness, emptiness, apathy, love, anger, guilt, sadness, fear, self-pity, and helplessness. These feelings have been described in this way:

> These feelings usher in the emotional freeze that covers solid ground with ice, making movement in any direction seem precarious and dangerous. Growth is hidden, progress seems blocked, and one bleakly speculates that just because the crocuses made it through the snow last year is no reason to believe they can do it again this year. It's not a pretty picture.[1]

A young wife shared with me how she felt when she found out that the baby she and her husband had been planning to adopt was going to be kept by the natural mother. "I felt as though something had been ripped right out of me. It hurt so bad. I felt hollow inside."

A divorced father shared with me, "For the past thirteen years, when my son has come to me for the weekend and I have to take him back to his mother, I grieve all over again. The pain comes back with all its intensity. It still cuts like a knife."

Does God understand our pain and our grief? In the early portion of Genesis we find the answer. Genesis 6:6 NAS says, "He was grieved in His heart."

When grief is your companion, you experience it psychologically through your feelings, thoughts, and attitudes. It impacts you socially as you interact with others. You experience it physically as it affects your health and is expressed in bodily symptoms.

Grief encompasses a number of changes. It appears differently at various times, and it flits in and out of your life. It is a natural, normal, predictable, and expected reaction. It is not an abnormal response. In fact, just the opposite is true. The absence of grief is abnormal. Grief is your own personal experience. Your loss does not have to be accepted or validated by others for you to experience and express grief.[2]

Why grief? Why do we have to go through this experience? What is the purpose? Grief responses express basically three things:

Through grief you express your feeling about your loss.

Through grief you express your protest at the loss as well as your desire to change what happened and have it not be true.

Through grief you express the effects you have experienced from the devastating impact of the loss.[3]

The purpose of grieving over your loss is to get beyond these reactions to face your loss and work on adapting to it. The overall purpose of grief is to bring you to the point of making necessary changes so you can live with the loss in a healthy way. It is a matter of beginning with the question, "Why did this happen to me?" and eventually moving on to, "How can I learn through this experience? How can I now go on with my life?" When the "How?" question replaces the "Why?" question, you have started to live with the reality of the loss. "Why?" questions reflect a search for meaning and purpose in loss. "How?" questions reflect your searching for ways to adjust to the loss.[4]

Your eventual goal is to be able to say:

> This loss I've experienced is a crucial upset in my life. In fact, it is the worst thing that will ever happen to me. But is it the end of my life? No. I can still have a rich and fulfilling life. Grief has been my companion and has taught me much. I can use it to grow into a stronger person than I was before my loss.[5]

> Mourning is the necessary process of returning back to life after we have been jolted from its road. It involves leaving behind what needs to be left behind, bringing along what needs to be brought along, and learning to distinguish between the two.[6]

What do you have to do to get to this point? Are there any definite steps you can take so you don't have to guess at the process? There are four steps that can be followed for most types of losses.

First of all, you need to change your relationship with whatever you lost. For example, if it was a person, you eventually need to come to the realization that the person is dead and you are no longer married to or dating him or her. You need to recognize the change and develop new ways of relating to the deceased person. You must learn to exist *without* the person the way you once learned to exist *with* the person. Memories, both positive and negative, will remain with you. Perhaps we can call this acknowledging and understanding the loss.

The next step is to develop your own self and your life to encompass and reflect the changes that occurred because of your loss. This will vary, depending upon whether the loss involved a job, an opportunity, a relationship, or the loss of a parent or spouse to death.

The third step is discovering and taking on new ways of existing and functioning without whatever it was you lost. This involves a new identity, but without totally forgetting.

Finally, you discover new directions for the emotional investments you once had in the lost object, situation, or person.[7]

These steps may sound simple but they are not, since all of grief involves work, effort, and pain. Let's consider how these steps can be accomplished.

Acknowledging and understanding the loss is essential to starting the grieving process. Depending upon the severity, some losses will soon be a faint memory whereas others, such as the death of a child or spouse, may never be completely settled. But this step does mean integrating the loss into your life.

You must overcome your shock and denial and face the painful reality of what occurred. It means saying, ''Yes, unfortunately this did happen.'' Facing your loss means you don't attempt to postpone the pain, you don't deny that it actually happened, and you don't minimize your loss.

If you do any of these, you intensify your pain and drag it out. It may be helpful to admit that you do want to postpone, deny, or minimize your loss. These are normal protective responses. A most common myth of grieving is that we should bury our feelings. Expressions such as, ''Don't cry,'' or ''Don't feel bad, after all, he's with the Lord now,'' or ''Don't feel bad, you can handle it,'' are damaging myths. Often they are expressions made by people who feel anxious when a loss occurs because they have never learned what to say. No matter what the reason, these are nonsupportive statements.

To assist in the process, it may help to make a list of the effects of your loss. This is one step in facing your pain. Feel and face all of your emotions. One author suggests that, "grieving means allowing yourself to feel your feelings, think your thoughts, lament your loss and protest your pain."[8]

Another step in the process of facing loss is to tell others about it as soon as possible. Call it by its name: "It was a loss and I am grieving." You may want to keep track of who you told, the date, and their response. Some have found it helpful to tell at least one or two people each day during the first week after the loss. It means making the conscious decision that "I am going to face it and feel the pain." The best way to describe this kind of pain is intense emotional suffering. You are going home to the uninvited guests of anger, denial, fear, anxiety, rage, depression, and many other emotions.

Sometimes people say they wish they could return to the initial stage of shock or numbness. At least at that point, the pain wasn't so intense. The numbness served as novocaine. "Numbness has been defined as 'devoid of sensation, devoid of emotion.' The exploding bombshell puts many people into a daze."[9]

Depending on the severity of your loss, your numb reaction can be a slight down feeling or an incapacitating numbness. Twenty-four to thirty-six hours later it lifts, the pain is faced, and the feelings surge like the seasons of the year. There are seasons of depression, anger, calm, fear, and eventually, hope, but they don't follow one another progressively. They overlap and are often jumbled together. Just when you think you are over one, it comes bursting through your door again. You finally smile, but then the tears return. You laugh, but the cloud of depression drifts in once again. This is normal. This is necessary. This is healing.

> The griever's suffering is never constant. The waves of
> pain are alternated by lulls of momentary rest. Initially, of
> course, in acute grief situations the waves are intense and

frequent. Gradually, as one is healed the waves are less frequent, less intense, less prolonged and less frequent. One can almost imagine the wave patterns charted on a graph, like radio waves. Each peak represents a mountain of pain, each valley a restful lull. Initially, the peaks are high and long, the valleys are narrow and short, and the frequency is high. Slowly, the peaks mellow, the valleys lengthen and the frequency decreases. Gradually, ever so gradually, the storm quiets. Yet months and years later an isolated wave can still come crashing ashore. On sentimental holidays, for example, the memories of lost loved ones are often raw. "Every Christmas," says a widowed, middle-aged woman, "after all the busyness is over, I sit down and have a good cry." Periodically, an isolated wave of grief washes against the shore of one's soul.[10]

Robert Veninga says, "There is one marvelously redeeming motive for entering fully into one's sorrow. Once you have experienced the seriousness of your loss, you will be able to experience the wonder of being alive."[11]

I recently read one of the most graphic and sad descriptions of what results when one does not share grief. This example was in a novel by Frederick Forsyth titled *The Negotiator*. The President's son had been kidnapped. The father had experienced the trauma of not knowing where his son was, what condition he was in, or whether he would ever be freed. But then the son was brutally murdered. After this occurrence, cabinet members were worried about the President. He sat and stared into space. He was described in this way: "Too introverted a man to share easily, too inhibited to express his grief, he had settled into an abiding melancholy that was sapping his mental and moral strength, those qualities humans call the will."[12]

Tears are the vehicle that God has equipped us with to express the deepest feelings words cannot express. One of the most gifted writers of our time, Max Lucado, has graphically portrayed the significance of tears in a chapter titled, "Hidden Messengers":

> Before we bid goodbye to those present at the cross, I have one more introduction to make. This introduction is very special.
>
> There was one group in attendance that day whose role was critical. They didn't speak much, but they were there. Few noticed them, but that's not surprising. Their very nature is so silent they are often overlooked. In fact, the gospel writers scarcely gave them a reference. But we know they were there. They had to be. They had a job to do.
>
> Yes, this representation did much more than witness the divine drama; they expressed it. They captured it. They displayed the despair of Peter; they betrayed the guilt of Pilate and unveiled the anguish of Judas. They transmitted John's confusion and translated Mary's compassion.
>
> Their prime role, however, was with that of the Messiah. With utter delicacy and tenderness, they offered relief to his pain and expression to his yearning.
>
> Who am I describing? You may be surprised.
>
> Tears.
>
> Those tiny drops of humanity. Those round, wet balls of fluid that tumble from our eyes, creep down our cheeks, and splash on the floor of our hearts. They were there that day. They are always present at such times. They should be; that's their job. They are miniature messengers; on call twenty-four hours a day to substitute for crippled words. They drip, drop, and pour from the corner of our souls, carrying with them the deepest emotions we possess. They tumble down our faces with announcements that range from the most blissful joy to darkest despair.
>
> The principle is simple; when words are most empty, tears are most apt. [13]

Genesis 42–50 is the account of Joseph's reunion with his brothers and his father. In his first encounter with his brothers, he told them one of them would need to stay in Egypt. They became frightened over what might happen to them. As Joseph listened to them talking among themselves in his native language, his emotions surged to the surface and, "He turned away from them and began to weep" (Genesis 42:24 NIV). When his brothers returned to Egypt with their youngest brother, the Bible says, "Deeply moved at the sight of his brother, Joseph hurried out and looked for a place to weep." Eventually he was so out of control that he "went into his private room and wept there" (Genesis 43:30 NIV). He wept uncontrollably again when his brother Judah made an offer to spare his father any more pain (Genesis 45:2 NIV).

The fourth occasion was after Joseph revealed to his brothers and father who he was, as well as his plan to bring them all to Egypt to live with him. At that point, "He threw his arms around his brother Benjamin and wept, and Benjamin embraced him, weeping." And then, "He kissed all his brothers and wept over them" (Genesis 45:14, 15 NIV).

Three more times we have record of Joseph weeping: when his father arrived in Egypt, when his father died seventeen years later, and finally, when his brothers sent a message to him asking him to forgive them. The verse says, "When their message came to him, Joseph wept" (Genesis 50:17 NIV).

When words fail, tears are the messenger. Tears are God's gift to all of us to release our feelings. When Jesus arrived in Bethany following the death of Lazarus, He wept (John 11:35). Ken Gire described this situation so beautifully in *Incredible Moments With the Savior:*

> On our way to Lazarus' tomb we stumble on still another question. Jesus approaches the gravesite with the full assurance that he will raise his friend from the dead. Why then does the sight of the tomb trouble him?
>
> Maybe the tomb in the garden is too graphic a reminder

of Eden gone to seed. Of Paradise lost. And of the cold, dark tomb he would have to enter to regain it.

In any case, it is remarkable that *our* plight could trouble *his* spirit; that *our* pain could summon *his* tears.

The raising of Lazarus is the most daring and dramatic of all the Savior's healings. He courageously went into a den where hostility raged against him to snatch a friend from the jaws of death.

It was an incredible moment.

It revealed that Jesus was who he said he was—the resurrection and the life. But it revealed something else.

The tears of God.

And who's to say which is more incredible—a man who raises the dead . . . or a God who weeps?[14]

The problem with tears is you never know when they will emerge when you are grieving. As many have said, when you experience a major loss in your life, you end up being ambushed by grief. I understand this statement far better now than a year ago at this time. I just never know what will trigger it again.

One morning it happened in our worship service at Hollywood Presbyterian Church. The service focused on Pentecost. As the organ played, suddenly the sound of a brass quartet filled the air. Trumpets were a sound that brought a response from Matthew. He would look up and reflect an alertness or wonderment in his expression, as if to say, "Oh, that's something new."

The sound of the brass in the service brought back another memory: Matthew's joyful laughter. Several years ago, I decided to take up the trumpet (which lasted only a few years). This included the purchase of a horn and weekly lessons. During one of Matthew's visits home, I took out the trumpet and began to practice. He looked at me with an expression that said, "I don't believe what I'm hearing!" He listened to another squawk, threw back his head, and laughed harder than we had ever heard him laugh. Again and again, he laughed and giggled until we were all in stitches. My novice attempts to play had at least pleased Matthew. Needless to say, these memories brought the tears once again.

Another time, I was driving home and listening to Dr. Chuck Swindoll's radio program. During the message, he began to list the names of the disciples. When he said the name *Matthew,* it brought my sense of loss and sadness to the surface, where it stayed for several days. Who would have thought that would have happened!

Then there are times when my feelings are just flat. There is a low-grade numbness, and I wonder when the pain is going to hit again. Just three months after Matthew died, I had been very busy with work and projects. For several days, there had been very little feeling and no tears. As I shared with a client what had happened, the tears came to my eyes. As I sat with the parents of a profoundly disabled child, attempting to help them, the tears rose to the surface. I received a note from a friend who had lost his nineteen-year-old son in an accident more than four years before. When he said that at times the pain was still as fresh as if it had just happened, I wondered, *Will it be that way for us?* Again my eyes clouded over.

During this "dry time" as I refer to it, grief hit hard again. I was riding my exercycle and listening to a worship tape by Terry Clark. One of the songs was "I Remember." As I rode, I was working on our new catalog to be sent out to a mailing list of several thousand people who had attended our seminars over the years. I was wondering whether or not to mention anything about Matthew in this publication, since most of the people had heard our story about him. I had thought of saying, "For years we had prayed for Matthew to be whole. On March 15, God saw fit to make him whole." As I thought about this (and perhaps because of the music and the fact that I was planning to visit his grave for the first time), the flood occurred. The sense of loss was overwhelming, and I wept intensely and audibly. I was still sobbing as I went into the other room, and Joyce heard me. Without a word, she came and held me and hugged me. Again, in the silence of grief, we found support and comfort from that brief embrace. Words were not needed; touch was. Our mutual tears had a language all their own.

Some of us have never learned to cry. We are afraid to really let go with our tears. We live with fears and reservations about crying. We cry on the inside but never on the outside. A way to overcome this is through the process of developing what is called a ''Programmed Cry.'' This is not a one-time activity but something a person might use on a number of occasions, especially during the first few months after a major loss.

Select a room in your house that has some sentimental value for you. You will need tissues, a stereo, and photographs of the person you lost, whether through a dating breakup, divorce, or death. It is best if this exercise is done in the evening.

The lights should be turned down low and the phone should be off the hook so there are no interruptions. Turn on the stereo to either tapes or a radio station that plays mellow music with few interruptions. As you begin to feel sad, continue to think about your loss. Look at any of the photographs that help you remember what you once had or would have had. Recall the positive and intimate times. Express out loud what you are feeling, and don't put a restraint on your tears.

Sometimes it helps to put an empty chair in front of you and talk to the chair as if the person were there. Talk to God out loud about the loss. Tears and words can express feelings of sadness, depression, longing, anger, hurt, fear, and frustration.

Remember that, in the midst of these feelings and their expression, a healing and recovery are taking place. As you begin to feel better, allow that healing to occur. Focus on the positive feelings and thoughts that emerge, and say the thoughts aloud. Then put away all the reminders and symbols of your weeping. Share your experience with a trusted friend or write it in a diary.

You will probably discover that your fear or resistance to crying has diminished. It will be easier the next time.[15]

A healthy response to a loss involves feelings of depression after the initial shock wears off. The loss is responded to both consciously and unconsciously by the brain and it is also influenced by previous experiences of loss. Depression begins to develop, and the depth of it depends upon the intensity of attachment we had to what was lost. Eventually the depression levels out and we begin to recover.

But a person who has had excessive losses in his life and has not learned to grieve properly may have developed negative patterns of thinking. This may cause him to hold on to the loss or continually re-create it. Pessimism will continue to re-create a loss. Some people have been taught, ''Don't hope and you won't be disappointed'' or ''Expect the worst and protect yourself.'' This is one of the ways to create the ''runaway train'' syndrome of depression. Leaving a train parked on a downgrade without the brakes properly set leads to some predictable consequences. As the train moves down the tracks, it picks up momentum and is soon out of control.

Sometimes depression gathers this same momentum because of guilt, self-blame, negative self-talk, distortions of reality, misperceptions, and imagining additional losses. The depression becomes self-perpetuating because we give it fuel. A college student who fails a major exam thinks, *I'll never pass this course, I don't have any ability, I didn't study the right way, I won't graduate, I won't get the job I want, My parents will think I'm a failure,* and so on. In time, this line of thinking would create depression in any of us. But the depression becomes disproportionate to the loss.

Some losses are very painful, and there is a normal depressive response. The depression is there for a purpose: to help us experience the loss and to recover from it.[16]

Recovery from loss is tied to our feelings. When they are not admitted, faced, and expressed, they become concealed. Withheld feelings lead to brittleness, vulnerability, and distorted perceptions.

Numerous studies have shown that your health risk is higher following a loss. You are more susceptible to heart attacks and cancer following the death of a loved one. A long-term study indicated that the death rate of widows and widowers is from two to seventeen times higher during the first year after the death of a spouse.[17]

Dr. Glen Davidson has discovered that about 25 percent of those who mourn experience a dramatic decrease in the body's immune system six to nine months following their loss. This is one of the reasons for the increase in illness when grieving. But if one does the work of grieving and doesn't postpone or avoid it, this immune system deficiency is avoidable.[18]

The pain from a loss generates numerous feelings. One of these is anxiety. *Anxiety* is *pain in the future* and includes a wide variety of fears and worries. These can be related to things and experiences in the past or future. Some people who haven't yet experienced their loss in reality experience it in their thoughts, and the dread that comes upon them is often as strong as if it had occurred.

Anxiety can be beneficial if you ask yourself what you are afraid of and why this is so important to you. Then steps can be taken to prevent or minimize the loss.

Hurt is a core feeling of loss. It is *pain in the present*. What does it feel like? Sometimes it is sadness, sometimes disappointment, and sometimes depression. It feels as if you have been depleted. You are drained. You need to cope with hurt by expressing it.

Anger is a response to the pain. It can be *pain in the past, present, or future*. When it is in the past, it is resentment. When direct expression is blocked, it leaks out and is invested elsewhere. If it is invested against oneself, it can become depression.

Have you ever tried to postpone the pain of a loss by creating a buffer against it? Often a person will use some sort of defense to gain time to adjust to the loss.

Some people become experts with mental gymnastics. These are mental games or tricks that we employ to deny, avoid, or defer an experience of loss. We are very much like ancient warriors who used shields to defer the attacks of enemy soldiers. In this case, our enemy is loss. We attempt to shield ourselves from the pain, but we never defeat the enemy through these efforts. We simply prolong its accompanying pain.

There are five different ways we attempt to negate the pain of our loss. The first defense against loss is *denial*. When the loss is that of rejection, abandonment, the loss of love, or even a death, denial is the usual defense. Often, people actually say, ''No! That's not true. It can't be true!''

Denial is a common companion to loss. In fact, some people choose to live in a world of denial most of their lives. Those who come from extremely dysfunctional families are gifted at this. When they deny, they avoid emotionally realizing that a loss has occurred or is going to occur. The most serious kind of loss is not only denying the reality of what has occurred but also the effects of that loss. Everything is blotted out of a person's mind at this time. I have seen denial in cases of loss of jobs, pets, persons, and even opportunities to go on to graduate school.

Denial comes in many shapes and forms. I have talked to people who say, ''Norm, I know up here in my head that this happened, but I feel as if it hasn't happened.'' It is as though they went to an anesthesiologist and received an injection for their feelings. They found the switch to turn off their emotions. In time, though, their emotions will catch up with their thoughts.

Another variation of denial is admitting the loss and feeling it but behaving as if it had never occurred. Some have called this ''third degree denial,'' and it is quite mild. Many people live their lives as if a loss did not occur. If you ask them about it, they can talk about it and even shed tears over what happened. But their behavior appears contrary to what happened.

Denial has its place and purpose. As author Joyce Landorf says:

> We need denial but we must not linger in it. We must recognize it as one of God's most unique tools and use it. Denial is our special oxygen mask to use when the breathtaking news of death has sucked every ounce of air out of us. It facilitates our bursting lungs by giving them their first gulps of sorrow-free air. We breathe in the breath of denial and seem to maintain life. We do not need to feel guilty or judge our level of Christianity when we clutch the mask to our mouth. However, after breathing has been restored and the initial danger has passed, we need not be dependent upon it.
>
> I think God longs for us to lay down the oxygen mask of denial, and with His help begin breathing into our lungs the fresh, free air of acceptance on our own.[19]

Grieving is moving through several levels of denial. Each stage brings home the reality of the loss a bit deeper and more painfully. We accept it first in our heads, then in our feelings, and finally we adjust life's pattern to reflect the reality of what has occurred. There is a price to pay for prolonged denial. The energy that must be expended to keep denial operating drains us, and in time we can be damaged emotionally, delaying our recovery.

Denial is used to block out the unthinkable, but it brings with it the fear of the unknown since you are denying the reality of what happened. As denial lessens, the pain begins to settle in and as it does, the fear of the unknown diminishes. Excuses are used when the loss is measured rather than felt. Rationalizing, justifying, or blaming others for your loss are the usual excuses.

Those who are used to being in control tend to use excuses. It is difficult for them to accept responsibility for their disappointments.

Rationalization is the second defense against loss. I often hear from clients, ''It really didn't hurt that bad. There are better men out there. After all, I only went with him for two years.'' Or, ''That job wasn't the best,'' ''Who needs a BMW?'' ''Our neighborhood was changing anyway,'' ''Well, she lived a good, long life and now she won't have to suffer anymore.'' Each of these statements has one basic purpose: to help the person cope with the pain of the loss. He or she wants to lessen its impact. But if a person lives with rationalization too long, he begins to believe it. It becomes a castle of protection to avoid the healing process.

A third defense we use to handle loss is *idealization*. This is another way to distort reality by idealizing what we lost. Any negative characteristics or aspects are overlooked, whether we are dealing with the loss of a job, death of a family member, or an unwanted divorce. An adolescent made this comment about his alcoholic, physically abusive father, who had recently died: ''Dad was really a good provider for all of us, and in his own way he really loved us.''

Perhaps we all tend to idealize a bit. In the process of grief, this soon recedes, which is necessary to create an accurate picture of the loss that has occurred. Sometimes idealization is so extreme that the grieving person will not allow anyone else to say anything bad or even realistic about the situation. Even when objective facts are shared by others, there is no acceptance.

A fourth defense is what we call *reaction formation*. The easiest way to explain this is to say it involves doing the opposite. When there is a loss, the person tends to run from his pain by overemphasizing the opposite of the present or impending pain.

Have you ever faced an impending loss and tried to keep it from occurring by overreacting? It is one thing for a student who is facing some failing grades to buckle down and study to change the impending loss. That is positive. But locking himself in his room, studying twelve hours a day, and missing meals and sleep is an overreaction. Fearing the loss of a person, one might become an overcompliant, submissive victim in a desperate attempt to hold on.

Many parents use this approach with their children without realizing what they are doing. It is a threatening experience to see children they were close to shift their allegiance to friends and peers during adolescence. To counter that impending loss, many parents become restrictive instead of allowing more independence. Unfortunately, this usually backfires and the adolescents rebel, stay away, and become devious to get what they want.

The final defense against loss that is sometimes used by adults and most of the time by young children is *regression*. This is a way of avoiding pain by retreating to a younger way of behaving or even thinking. Regressive responses are even more ineffective than are normal ways of responding.

If regression or any of these defense mechanisms become permanent fixtures in our lives, the pain is not eliminated but simply locked in as a barrier to growth and recovery. Recovery comes through facing the loss and grieving. There is no other way.[20]

There is one vital thing that must be remembered: you desperately need the support, help, and comfort of other people during your loss. You may think this is only necessary in the major losses of life. However, you need support in the smaller losses as well: a broken relationship, a child not being accepted into your alma mater, a lost pet, having your house fall out of escrow, taking third place in a competition, and so on.

Isolation during a loss can be deadly. A friend or even an acquaintance can help you walk through the valley, take away your fear of abandonment, and assist in lifting the depression. Other people can help you see that you *can* continue to function. It is as if they loan their hope and faith when yours has vanished. This is why so many people are involved in self-help groups. The

U.S. Public Health Service has stated that, in the 1970s, fifteen million people in this country were members of over five hundred thousand support groups. This number has increased since that time.

You may know intellectually that being with people is the best thing for you, but emotionally you don't want to be with them. It may help to talk about your feelings with a nonjudgmental, caring, listening friend. It may be helpful to write down everything you are feeling and then express it. This is not a one-time experience. You will need to do it again and again and again. Some people talk, run, walk fast, talk softly, scream, draw, pound on a bed—you have many forms of expression open to you. The feelings will last for some time.

Jan and Ed were a couple who lost their seven-year-old son. They shared an experience that happened in the year following his death:

> The first Christmas after Mark died, a neighbor Jan knew only slightly telephoned. She must have realized how difficult Christmas would be for Jan and Ed after losing their elder son. "I don't know if I should call," she said, "but I was just thinking you won't be buying Mark any presents this year. . . ." The neighbor suddenly stopped talking and started crying.
>
> Jan responded, saying, "It must have taken a lot of courage to call and say that." Now weeping also, Jan explained, "I'm not crying because your words hurt me but because it's a gift that you are remembering Mark."[21]

A *Los Angeles Times* article told the story of an elderly woman who called a grief hot line. She had lost her husband of fifty-five years a year ago around Christmastime, and now at the holidays her children had invited her to visit them. But she was afraid to cry in front of them because she didn't want another lecture on how to live her life without her husband. They kept telling her that she should be fine now because it had been a year since his death.

The counselor asked her to share with him some information about her husband. She told about their first Christmas and the little tree they bought because they were so poor. He also asked her to share a funny incident about her husband, which brought some laughter to both of them. The counselor then worked out a sentence for her to say whenever she was feeling her loss: "There will be times during these holidays that I will miss my husband. I will cry. And when I do, I don't need to be fixed because there is nothing wrong with me."[22] This is a statement we all need to remember: When I am crying I don't need to be fixed because there is nothing wrong with me!

During our time of grief over the death of our son, people would ask us how we were doing. We would say, "We're doing fine. We're grieving, crying, and feeling the loss." The additional words were to let them know just what "doing fine" actually meant, since they might otherwise assume the tears had gone.

You may be uncomfortable with your grief. So might others around you. They want you "normal" as soon as possible, or they want you to act as if you are. But you are not ready for it, and others should not be the ones to determine when you are ready. This is your loss, not theirs. No one should rob you of your grief. Some may attempt to do just that because they are uncomfortable. Years ago, anthropologist Margaret Mead said, "When a person is born we celebrate; when they marry we jubilate; but when they die we act as if nothing has happened."[23]

When births occur and marriages take place, loss is involved. But the losses are dominated by joyful gain. Most of us know what to say and how to react on those occasions. But death is seen as a closed door to the existence of human joy.

Life is a mixture of pain and joy. This is the time of pain. The seriousness of your loss and what you need is understood best in the context of your perspective. Only you know what this loss means to you.

What most of us don't realize is the pattern of peaks and valleys of grief. Look at the intensity of grief as indicated by this chart:[24]

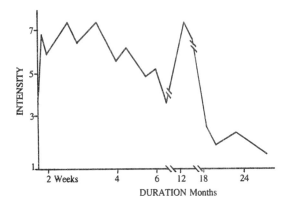

Notice the jagged peaks. The pain and grief actually intensify at three months and then gradually subside, but not in a steady fashion. They go up and down. Most people don't need a reminder of the first-year anniversary of the loss of a loved one. The intensity of grief comes rushing in with pain that rivals the initial feelings of loss. If anyone attempts to tell you that you should be "over it by now" or "feeling better" at any of these times, you may become quite upset with them. That is understandable. It is also understandable that people lack an understanding of the process of grief unless they have been through it themselves. Share this chart with them and let them know how you are feeling and how normal it is.

It is all right for you to take charge and let others know what you need and don't need at this time of your life. That doesn't always mean that others will comply, but they can try. Unfortunately you may have to educate them about grief. You have to go after what you need to resolve your loss. Let others know that they don't have to avoid bringing up your loss. Let them know you want them to call, to ask you how you are doing, and not be put off by your tears or anger.

Perhaps it would help you and others if you prepared a set of instructions to ease their anxiety and assist you by responding in the most helpful fashion. Here is a suggested letter that can be altered to fit your loss situation:

Dear Friend (family, pastor, fellow workers . . .)

Recently I have suffered a devastating loss. I am grieving and it will take months and even years to recover from this loss.

I wanted to let you know that I will cry from time to time. I don't apologize for my tears since they are not a sign of weakness or a lack of faith. They are God's gift to me to express the extent of my loss, and they are also a sign that I am recovering.

At times you may see me angry for no apparent reason. Sometimes I'm not sure why. All I know is that my emotions are intense because of my grief. If I don't always make sense to you, please be forgiving and patient with me. And if I repeat myself again and again, please accept this as normal.

More than anything I need your understanding and your presence. You don't always have to know what to say or even say anything if you don't know how to respond. Your presence and a touch or hug lets me know you care. Please don't wait for me to call you since sometimes I am too tired or tearful to do so.

If I tend to withdraw from you, please don't let me do that. I need you to reach out to me for several months.

Pray for me that I would come to see meaning in my loss someday and that I would know God's comfort and love. It does help to let me know that you are praying for me.

If you have experienced a similar type of loss, please feel free to share it with me. It will help rather than cause me to feel worse. And don't stop sharing if I begin to cry. It's all right, and any tears you express as we talk are all right too.

This loss is so painful, and right now it feels like the worst thing that could ever happen to me. But I will survive and eventually recover. I cling to that knowledge, even though there have been times when I didn't feel it. I know that I will not always feel as I do now. Laughter and joy will emerge once again someday.

Thank you for caring about me. Thank you for listening and praying. Your concern comforts me and is a gift for which I will always be thankful.[25]

Take charge of your grief. Face it. Experience it and you will recover.

Notes

Chapter 3 The Meaning of Grief

1. Lilly Singer, Margaret Sirot, and Susan Rodd, *Beyond Loss* (New York: E. P. Dutton, 1988), 62.

2. Therese A. Rando, *Grieving: How to Go On Living When Someone You Love Dies* (Lexington, Massachusetts: Lexington Books, 1988), 11, 12, adapted.

3. Ibid., 18, 19, adapted.

4. Bob Deits, *Life After Loss* (Tucson: Fisher Books, 1988), 27, adapted.

5. Ibid., 28, adapted.

6. James Froehlich, O.F.M. Cap, in a paper written for the Pastoral Helping Relationship graduate course at Loyola College, Baltimore: 1984.

7. Rando, *Grieving*, 19, adapted.

8. Ibid., 242.

9. Robert Veninga, *A Gift of Hope* (Boston: Little, Brown and Company, 1985), 15, adapted.

10. R. Scott Sullender, *Grief and Growth* (New York: Paulist Press, 1985), 56.

11. Veninga, *Gift of Hope*, 71.

12. Frederick Forsyth, *The Negotiator* (New York: Bantam Books, 1989), 269.

13. Max Lucado, *No Wonder They Call Him the Savior* (Portland, Oregon: Multnomah Press, 1986), 105, 106.

14. Ken Mire, *Incredible Moments With the Savior* (Grand Rapids, Michigan: Zondervan Publishing House, 1990), 96, 97, adapted.

15. Deits, *Life After Loss*, 144–146, adapted.

16. Archibald Hart, *Counseling the Depressed* (Waco, Texas: Word Books, 1987), 78–84, adapted.

17. Deits, *Life After Loss*, 103, adapted.

18. Glen W. Davidson, *Understanding Mourning* (Minneapolis: Augsburg Publishing House, 1984), 24–27, adapted.

19. Joyce Landorf, *Mourning Song* (Old Tappan, New Jersey: Fleming H. Revell Company, 1974), 63.

20. R. Scott Sullender, *Losses in Later Life* (New York: Paulist Press, 1989), 7–10, adapted.

21. Ann Kaiser Stearns, *Coming Back* (New York: Ballantine Books, 1988), 16, 17.

22. Michael Quinta Nilla, "Hot Line Has Solace for the Grieving," *Los Angeles Times*, adapted.

23. As quoted in Deits, *Life After Loss*, 148.

24. Davidson, *Understanding Mourning*, 59.

25. Deits, *Life After Loss*, 150, 151, adapted by permission of the author as given in his book.

4

Problems in Grieving and Recovery

There are occasions when the recovery from a loss is disturbed for one reason or another. This is usually referred to as "unresolved grief." There are many reasons for this, and some of them may overlap. In each case, you will find some denial or repression and an attempt to hold on to whatever was lost.

Absent grief is just what it sounds like. Feelings of grief and mourning over the loss cannot be found. It is as though the loss never occurred. There is a significant amount of denial in this response. Sometimes the person shows minimal signs of grief.

A minimizer is a person who is aware of feelings of grief but works to minimize the feelings, diluting them through a variety of rationalizations. The person attempts to prove that he or she is not really impacted by the loss that was experienced. Observers of minimizers may well hear them talk about how they are back to their normal routines.

On a conscious level, the minimizer may seem to be working and certainly conforming to society's message to quickly "get over" one's grief. However, internally the repressed feelings of grief continue to build and fester and, with no outlet, emotional strain and tension are the results.

This person often believes grief is something to be quickly *thought* through but not *felt*. This is typically an intellectual process in which words become a substitute for the expression of true feelings. Any feelings of grief are very threatening to the minimizer, who seeks to avoid pain at all costs.

Inhibited grief involves the repression of some of the normal grief responses. Other symptoms, such as somatic complaints, may take their place. Stomachaches, loss of energy, or headaches are some of the more common responses. The grieving person may be able to grieve only over certain aspects of what was lost. Perhaps he grieves for the positive aspects but not the negative ones.

A somatizer is a person who converts his or her feelings of grief into physical symptoms. This converted physical expression of grief can range from relatively benign minor complaints to the severely chronic pattern of multiple vague somatic complaints with no physical basis.

Unfortunately, many grieving people unconsciously adopt this somatizer role in an effort to get their emotional needs met. By taking on the "sick role," their very real need to be nurtured and comforted is legitimized by people around them. These persons often fear that if they were to express their true feelings of grief, people would pull away and leave them feeling abandoned.

Sometimes grief is *delayed* for an extended period of time, which could mean months or in some cases even years. It could be because of an overload of pressing responsibilities, or perhaps the grieving person feels he just can't deal with the grief at that time. When grief over a loss is delayed, some other loss in the future may trigger its release and it may come like an avalanche. Even a very small future loss can be the catalyst to release the past grief.

A person who delays grief is called a postponer. He or she believes that if you delay the expression of grief, it will go away. Obviously, it does not. The grief builds within and typically comes out in a variety of ways that are not good for the mourner.

This individual may feel that if the grief doesn't vanish, at least at some point in time he or she will feel safer in experiencing the pain. Unaware that through expression comes healing, he continues to postpone. The grief builds up inside the person, pushing toward the point of explosion, thus making him feel even less capable of experiencing feelings related to the loss. It is an unfortunate choice for handling grief.

Roy Fairchild's statement on delayed grief is very insightful:

> The refusal to mourn is the refusal to say goodbye to beloved persons, places, missed opportunities, vitality, or whatever has been "taken away"; which is how many religious people view these losses. The refusal to mourn our earlier disappointments condemns us and rigidifies us, as it did Lot's wife. Genuine grief is the deep sadness and weeping that expresses the acceptance of our inability to do anything about our losses. It is a prelude to letting go, to relinquishment. It is dying that precedes resurrection. Our sadness reveals what we have been invested in; it is the cost of a commitment which has been shattered.[1]

Some people experience *conflicted* grief in which there can be an exaggeration of some of the characteristics of normal grief while other aspects that should also be present are suppressed. Sometimes in grieving over a loved one, this reaction occurs because of having had either a dependent or ambivalent relationship with the person.

Another major problem grief response is *displacing* the grief. The displacer is the person who takes the expression of grief away from the actual loss and channels the feelings in other directions. For example, while not acknowledging feelings of grief, the person may complain of difficulty at work or in relationships with other people. Another example is the person who appears to be chronically agitated and upset at even the most minor events. While some awareness may be present, displacing usually occurs with no conscious awareness.

Some individuals who are displacers become bitter toward life in general. Others displace the bitter, unconscious expression of their grief inward and become full of self-hate, experiencing a crippling depression. At times, these people displace their grief in interactions with other people; at other times they believe people dislike them. Then once again they project unhappiness from within themselves to others.

The purpose of displacing is to shift grief away from its source and on to a less-threatening person, place, or situation. Personal relationships often become stressed and strained for the displacer, who is unable to acknowledge the occurrence of this common pattern of grief avoidance.

Chronic grief is a response in which a person continues to show grief responses that were appropriate in the early stages of grief. The mourning continues and doesn't proceed to any sign of closure. It appears that the person is keeping the loss alive with grief. This is especially prevalent in the loss of a person, when the relationship was very intense, with a great deal of emotional investment.

When a loss occurs within a family, it creates a major crisis. The family has been accustomed to functioning according to certain routines. Each person has his or her role, and this is crucial to the organization and functioning of the family unit. A family unit gives protection and meaning to the members. Each person finds his own identity within the family and comes to understand that he is a separate individual.

When a family member is taken by death, there is an enormous vacuum within that family. The balance is disrupted. Not only are roles affected but each person's identity as well. A death forces each person to make some significant adjustments in his or her own role and the way he responds to the other family members. The giving of love, comfort, and support may be a new role for some of the members, but the need for it is quite significant.

New roles have to be hammered out for each person, but before that can occur, they all need time and space to understand and handle the loss in their own way. One person might withdraw too much and become isolated unless brought back. Another may try to smother the others because of some of their fears. The new roles will have to be felt out until the family learns to function once again as a unit.[2]

A recent classification of grief is called *unanticipated* grief. This can be seen when there has been a sudden, unanticipated loss that, like a crushing blow, leaves a person devastated. It is such a shock that the person is unable to grasp the totality of what has happened. He or she has difficulty accepting the loss because his capabilities for doing so have been damaged.

In her excellent book *Helping People Through Grief*, Delores Kuenning writes:

> The impact of sudden death is devastating, for it happens without warning or a chance to anticipate what lies ahead. It allows no time for goodbyes, no time to make amends or ask forgiveness for harsh words spoken in trivial quarrels, and no time to express the love one feels but doesn't verbalize. The unfinished business of the day can never be transacted—it remains unresolved. It is like an unfinished song, the melody stopped in mid-phrase that longs for completion.[3]

In *Grief, Dying, and Death*, Therese A. Rando says about sudden death:

> At least when a death has been anticipated, even though it puts tremendous emotional demands on the individuals

involved, coping capacities are directed toward an expectable end. When the loss occurs, it has been prepared for. When this preparation is lacking, and the loss comes from out of the blue, grievers are shocked. They painfully learn that major catastrophic events can occur without warning. As a result, they develop a chronic apprehension that something unpleasant may happen at any time. It is this lack of security, along with the experience of being overwhelmed and unable to grasp the situation, that accounts for the severe postdeath bereavement complications that occur in cases of sudden death.[4]

In *Grief Counseling and Grief Therapy,* the author identifies seven special features that tend to complicate the grief process for survivors of a sudden-death experience:

1. Sudden death usually leaves the survivor with a sense of unreality that may last a long time.
2. Sudden death fosters a stronger-than-normal sense of guilt expressed in "if only . . ." statements.
3. In sudden death, the need to blame someone for what happened is extremely strong.
4. Sudden death often involves medical and legal authorities.
5. Sudden death often elicits a sense of helplessness on the part of the survivor.
6. Sudden death leaves the survivor with many regrets and a sense of unfinished business.
7. In the event of a sudden death, there is the need to understand why it happened. Along with this is the need to ascribe not only the cause but the blame. Sometimes God is the only available target and it is not uncommon to hear someone say, "I hate God."[5]

Whenever a close loved one dies unexpectedly, the last time you were together is very significant. You remember the last conversation, the last touch, and the surroundings. It stands out vividly. It is as though somebody hit the "freeze" button on the videocassette player, and the movie of your life froze at this last encounter. You tend to play it over and over again in your mind.

If your last memory was pleasant, it makes the grieving easier. That good memory helps to comfort you. But it doesn't always happen that way. You may have wanted to be with the person whenever he or she died, but the suddenness of the event robbed you of that opportunity. You may have wanted to say more to the person the last time you were together. Or your last encounter could have been an unpleasant conflict, and the relationship had not been fully restored yet. There is a feeling of unfinished business. Sometimes people say, "I'll call her tomorrow and straighten this out." But tomorrow never has a chance to arrive.

Sometimes these last unpleasant scenes tend to haunt a person. Your task then will be to soften the memories and images that hurt you so much. How do you do this? By doing some editing as if it were a movie. You can hang on to the hurting, negative images or choose to go back a bit further in time and dwell on a scene that is representative of your relationship and how you feel about that person overall. Let that scene be your source of comfort, since it more accurately represents the relationship you had.[6]

Abbreviated grief can be mistaken for unresolved grief. It is a normal grief response but very brief. There are several reasons for it: there could be an immediate replacement of what was lost, there wasn't that much attachment to what was lost, or, as in the case of a terminally ill person, much of the grieving occurs in advance of the death. Some people bypass the grieving with replacement.

A *replacer* is a person who takes the emotions that were invested in the relationship that ended in death and prematurely reinvests them in another relationship. For the most part, he or she is not conscious that the replacement efforts are really a means of avoiding facing and resolving grief.

Outsiders will sometimes assume the replacer must not have loved the person who died if he or she can so quickly become involved in a new relationship. In actuality, often the replacer has loved very much, and out of the need to overcome the pain of confronting feelings related to the loss, avoids the pain by replacement. Replacement can include not only a person but also excesses in other areas, such as overwork or plunging frantically into one's hobbies.

There are three primary characteristics of unresolved grief: (1) absence of a normal grief reaction; (2) a reaction that lingers; (3) a distortion of a normal grief reaction.

When you have one or more of these symptoms, and they continue beyond six months or a year, you may have unresolved grief. The likelihood of unresolved grief increases as the number of symptoms increases. Some of these symptoms are:

1. A pattern of depression that lingers and often is accompanied by guilt and lowered self-esteem.
2. A history of extended or prolonged grief that reflects an already existing difficulty with grief.
3. A wide variety of symptoms such as guilt, self-blame, panic attacks, feelings of choking, and fears.
4. Physical symptoms similar to those of the deceased person's terminal illness due to overidentification with the individual.
5. A restless searching for what was lost with a lot of purposeless, random behavior, and moving about.
6. Recurring depression that is triggered on specific dates such as anniversaries of the loss, birthday of a deceased person, holidays, and even becoming the same age as the person who died. When these reactions are more extreme than normal responses, it can be indicative of unresolved grief.
7. Feelings that the loss occurred yesterday, even though months or years have passed.
8. Enshrinement or unwillingness to remove the belongings of a deceased person after a reasonable period of time.

9. Changes in personal relationships with other significant people following the death.
10. Withdrawal from normal religious activities and the avoidance of usual mourning activities that are part of the person's culture.
11. Inability to talk about the loss without breaking down, especially when it occurred over a year before.
12. Extensive thinking about and noticing themes of loss in life.
13. Minor losses triggering major grief reactions.
14. Phobias about death or illness.
15. Excluding anything or anyone who used to be associated with a significant loss or deceased person.
16. A compulsion to imitate the deceased person due to over-identification with him or her.[7]

Why do some people move through grief so well while others have such struggles? Are there some common clues that can be identified? There are numerous factors that predispose a person to difficulty in resolving grief over a loss. We have to allow for variation of responses in grief, but for now we are considering recognizable unresolved grief.

One reason for unresolved grief is that a person is unable to handle the emotional pain of grief, so he tends to resist the process. Another reason might be that the individual has an excessive need to maintain interaction with the person who is no longer there. This can be true for divorce as well as losing someone in death.

Other reasons include the following:

Guilt can block grief. If we begin to reflect on our relationship with the person who is gone, we may experience excessive guilt over behaviors, feelings, or even neglect that occurred in the relationship. If we have very high standards regarding our interpersonal relationships, it may not take too much to activate our guilt. This in turn blocks the grieving, since we feel unable to confront our guilt.

Have you ever heard someone say, ''My life is a total loss without her. I feel like half a person. I cannot function without her.'' This could reflect an excessive dependence that in turn leads to an avoidance of grieving. This person tries to avoid the reality of the loss because part of the loss seems to be himself.

Some people resist grieving because the loss reactivates unresolved losses from the past that are even more painful to handle than the present one. Thus an endless pattern of postponing grieving is set into motion.

Overload may be another reason for unresolved grief. There are occasions in our lives when we experience a number of losses in a short period of time, and it is just too much to bear at one time. The losses are too heavy to face and handle. If a person loses several members of his family or even several friends at one time, not only does it produce overload but he has also lost some of the people who could have given him support and comfort as he grieves.

Some individuals have never fully and adequately developed their individual identity. They haven't matured sufficiently psychologically and emotionally, and whenever they are confronted with a loss, they tend to regress.

Still others fail to grieve because of misbeliefs they hold on to. They fear losing control, for they have been taught that losing control isn't proper. They do not want to appear weak to others and to themselves. Some do not want to give up their personal pain because it ties them closer to the person they lost.

Did you know that there are factors in society that actually hinder the grieving process? For example, there are numerous losses that occur which either are not recognized as losses or are not given the significance they deserve. The loss of a pet may not seem significant to friends or relatives of the person who incurred the loss, so they don't participate in or support the loss.

Several years ago, a friend of mine had to have his fourteen-year-old cat put to sleep, and he asked me to accompany him. He knew it would be traumatic and requested my presence to assist him in his grief and to give support. When our sheltie had to be taken to the vet in 1989 to be put to sleep, both my wife and I wept. Our friends knew that this would be difficult for us and they acknowledged the loss; their sensitivity helped us. However, not everyone has the benefit of support when a pet dies.

Abortion is a loss not only for the mother but for the father and potential grandparents as well. Who helps and encourages these people to grieve? A miscarriage is the death of a child just as much as the death of a ten-year-old is. But many times insufficient time and attention are given to a miscarriage situation. Giving a child up for adoption or finding out you can't have children are losses.

Some losses seem to be repulsive or basically unacceptable. Friends, relatives, and others don't want to even acknowledge them, let alone assist in the grieving process. Part of their struggle is, "What do I say at a time like this?"

How do you respond when a family member . . .

. . . dies of a cocaine overdose?

. . . takes his or her own life?

. . . is murdered by the husband of the woman with whom the deceased was involved?

. . . is imprisoned for embezzling funds from his job?

. . . is arrested for selling drugs and his father is the pastor of your church?

Feelings of distaste and disgust often block a person's ability to grieve or assist others in the process.

Sometimes people are simply isolated and lack other people to help them with the grieving process. Geographical distance could inhibit the process because of the mobility limitations of our society.

For example, a son of missionary parents was in the States at boarding school. The day he left on a five-day trip to see his parents on the mission field, his father died. By the time he arrived, the remaining family members had found comfort from one another in their grief and had passed through the shock phase. In addition, his father had to be buried immediately because of the primitive conditions and lack of mortuary facilities. So the son missed that experience as well.

Another reason grief is unresolved is our failure to teach people how to handle the losses of life and to grieve properly. There is a denial mentality in our society toward loss and death, and this attitude breeds its own set of problems.

When a family member, such as a father, dies, often one of the children assumes the role of "the strong one" and takes on the responsibility for all of the arrangements and details. This person is also expected to support and encourage the others and let them lean on him or her. This doesn't allow the person the opportunity to conduct his own grief work.

In our society, we give more support to widows than to widowers. But it is men who tend to have more difficulty than women in adjusting to the loss of a spouse:

> Widowers, especially young men, often experience the unrealistic societal expectations to "be strong" and take it "like a man." The male is expected to be more resilient and able to control his feelings. These expectations may inhibit a man from openly expressing his grief. It should be clearly understood that both men and women experience the shock, the anger, guilt and loneliness, and depression that accompanies bereavement. When forced to suffer in silence, a man's pain can become unbearable for him and produce an inner rage.[8]

> Traditionally, society has not understood the role, identity, and special plight of the widower. To the contrary, widowers must learn certain life skills such as purchasing children's clothing, doing laundry, buying food, preparing meals, learning household chores, and supporting grieving

children. Loneliness is the greatest problem suffered and many widowers admit they are tempted to find a female companion too soon in order to fill the void.[9]

Have you ever wondered how a person properly grieves over a loss when there is uncertainty over the loss? What do you do when a car or family heirloom is stolen, or when a son is missing in action, or when a father's boat is found on a lake following a storm, but he is not to be found? Perhaps you have wondered why people have searched for years for the MIAs from Vietnam or worked to have a soldier's body returned from a grave in North Vietnam, or why days are spent attempting to recover a body from a boating accident or a cave-in. One of the many reasons death needs to be confirmed is that it allows the survivors to begin the grieving process.[10]

What can you do when you are stuck in your grief? Perhaps the following suggestions will help because they will give you a sense of being in control of the situation. At least you can see yourself doing something about the problem. The chapter on recovery will give you a number of additional steps to follow.

1. Try to identify what it is that doesn't make sense to you about your loss. Perhaps it is a vague question about life or God's purpose for us. Or it could be a specific question: "Why did this have to happen to me now, at this crucial point in my life?" Ask yourself, "What is it that is bothering me the most?" Keep a card with you for several days to record your thoughts as they emerge.

2. Identify the emotions you feel during each day. Are you experiencing sadness, anger, regret, "if onlys," hurt, or guilt? What are the feelings directed at? Has the intensity of the feelings decreased or increased during the past few days? If your feelings are vague, identifying and labeling them will diminish their power over you.

3. State the steps or actions you are taking to help you move ahead and overcome your loss. Identify what you have done in the past that has helped or ask a trusted friend for help.

4. Be sure you are sharing your loss and grief with others who can listen to you and support you during this time. Don't seek out advice-givers but those who are empathetic and can handle your feelings. Remember, your journey through grief will never be exactly like that of another person; each of us is unique.

5. It may help to find a person who has experienced a similar loss. Groups and organizations abound for losses of all types. Reading books or stories about those who have survived similar experiences can be helpful.

6. Identify the positive characteristics and strengths of your life that have helped you before. Which of these will help you at this time in your life?

7. Spend time reading in the Psalms. Many of them reflect the struggle of human loss but give the comfort and assurance that are from God's mercies.

8. When you pray, share your confusion, your feelings, and your hopes with God. Be sure to be involved in the worship services of your church since worship is an important element in recovery and stabilization.

9. Think about where you want to be in your life two years from now. Write out some of your dreams and goals. Just setting some goals may encourage you to realize you will recover.

10. Become familiar with the stages of grief. Then you will know what to expect and you won't be thrown by what you are experiencing.

11. Remember that understanding your grief intellectually is not sufficient. It can't replace the emotional experience of living through this difficult time. You need to be patient and allow your feelings to catch up with your mind. Expect mood swings, and remind yourself of these through notes placed in obvious places. These mood swings are normal.

Notes

Chapter 4 Problems in Grieving and Recovery

1. Roy W. Fairchild, *Finding Hope Again: A Pastor's Guide to Counseling Depressed Persons* (San Francisco: Harper and Row, Publishers, 1980), 113, 114.

2. Lilly Singer, Margaret Sirot, and Susan Rodd, *Beyond Loss* (New York: E. P. Dutton, 1988), 82, 83, adapted.

3. Delores Kuenning, *Helping People Through Grief* (Minneapolis: Bethany House Publishers, 1987), 191.

4. Therese A. Rando, *Grief, Dying, and Death: Clinical Interventions for Caregivers* (Champaign, Illinois: Research Press, 1984), 52.

5. William Wordon, *Grief Counseling and Grief Therapy* (New York: Springer Publishing Company, 1982), 84, 85.

6. R. Scott Sullender, *Losses in Later Life* (New York: Paulist Press, 1989), 115, adapted.

7. Rando, *Grief, Dying, and Death*, 63, 64, adapted.

8. Kuenning, *Helping People Through Grief*, 217.

9. Louise A. Allen, "The Forgotten Man: Creative Approaches to Helping the Widower," *Thanatos* (Spring, Vol. 8, No. 1), 5.

10. Rando, *Grief, Dying, and Death*, 59–62, 64–67, adapted.

5

Adjusting to the Separation and Void

In addition to experiencing the pain of loss, you must also adjust to the void left by the person or object that is gone. Whether it is the loss of a dream, a job, a friend, a pet, or a spouse, there is an empty place in your life—a vacuum that nothing seems to fill. You must become accustomed to the absence of something that was a very important part of your life. The feeling of emptiness you experience will be directly related to the significance of what you lost. Your task now is to learn how to function without whatever is gone.

If your loss was a person, you learn to move on without that special relationship. This is the type of loss you will probably resist because it is not something you wanted. Even when a long-term close friend moves away, this kind of adjustment is necessary. You automatically go to the phone to give him or her a call or walk down the block to drop in, and then you realize the person is no longer there. A widow turns over in bed to put her arm around her husband, and the reality that he is no longer a part of her life hits her.

In the loss of a person, you have to learn how to function without the interaction and validation you were accustomed to

from that person. The lack of the person's physical presence in
your life means your needs, hopes, dreams, expectations, feelings, and thoughts will change. Slowly over time, the reality of
separation begins to sink in and you realize, "For now, I exist
without this person as a part of my life."

Even as I write these words, I still feel the freshness of my
son's death. We purchased a pumpkin for Halloween, but
Matthew won't be here this year to sit on it or have his picture taken with it. He won't be coming home for the Thanksgiving or Christmas holidays either. When those days arrive,
the lack of his presence will be felt. We must experience and
accept it.

Whatever loss you experienced, it means making changes.
Not being able to continue in school may mean major changes
in your time, future hopes, economic structure, other people's
expectations and perceptions of you, and your feelings about
yourself. An elderly person who loses a pet may experience
major grief, for perhaps her cat was the main companion in her
life. If you lost a person, you may discover it will take time to
identify all the ways this person was a part of your life. It is a
step-by-step process. The loss of companionship, how much
you depended upon the person, his or her opinions—all of these
are new and separate losses that make up the major loss of your
life.

Each time you start to respond to the person who is no longer
there, you discover again that he or she is *no longer there*. It is
a fact, and there will be many reminders. Even when a business
relationship dissolves, you may automatically turn to the person
to take care of a task usually handled for you—only to realize the
person is gone.

Whenever a significant person is lost from your life, you
have to broaden your roles and your skills and learn to function
without him or her. You learn to make up for what you lost.
You change what you do, take over responsibility, and find an-

other person to help. There will be some things you don't do anymore. Adjustment means and necessitates not behaving the same way you did when the person was a part of your world.

For many people, the loss of a significant person means acquiring a new identity. You will never be quite the same as you were before the loss. As one person said, "That portion of my life is history. I will never be that way or be that person again." Look at the people around you and think about how their losses were turning points in their lives. Often people point to the time of loss as a turn in the road for the direction of their lives. My mother, who is ninety-one years old, lost her first husband when she was thirty-four. When she was sixty-one, her second husband (my father) was killed in an automobile accident. Major changes in her life occurred after each of these events.

Perhaps the most crucial task to be completed is developing a new relationship with what it was you lost. With some losses, this is relatively easy and clean since in a short time there is a diminishing emotional effect of the loss. A lost opportunity, job, competition, pet, a wrecked car, or a stolen wallet may not have the same lasting effect as some other experiences. One of the most difficult is a divorce situation in which children are involved and one of the spouses did not want the divorce. Because of the children, there is a continuing relationship over the years and a constant experiencing of past, present, and future losses.

Getting on with your life involves several steps, some of which may come as a surprise to you. Few people are aware of them before they experience a major loss. Some, unfortunately, either resist these steps or become stuck in their grief work. Sometimes after people have gone through these stages, they are able to sit down and identify what they have experienced. But what a difference it can make in your life if you are aware of the process in advance. It doesn't necessarily lessen the pain, but it gives you a direction and lets you know you are on track and you are not going crazy. These steps apply to the more serious and impacting losses.

You will need to develop some type of new relationship with what you lost, especially in a divorce situation or the death of a spouse or child, and for purposes of this discussion, we are going to consider death or divorce as the loss.

The change involves keeping the loved one alive in your memory in a healthy and appropriate manner. Formation of a new identity without this person's presence in your life is another step that needs to be completed.

As these steps are in process and your grief work is being completed, the emotional energy that was once invested in the person you lost is now freed up and reinvested in other people, activities, and hopes that in turn can give emotional satisfaction back to you.

How do you develop a new relationship with the one you lost? In a divorce, often this is worked out by the courts. That is fairly easy to understand. But what do you do about a spouse or child you lost through death? Death ends the person's life but not your relationship. This is not morbid or pathological. It is a very normal response. But who openly talks about it? Have you ever heard a discussion about such a relationship being normal? Probably not. And if you bring it up for discussion, people might look at you as if you were involved in New Age thinking! But if people tell you that the best way to deal with your loss is to forget the person, they are inhibiting your grief experience. That is the absolute truth.

We keep people alive all the time, as we reflect upon who they were, their achievements, and their impact upon society. I have heard a number of people make the statement, ''I wonder what he would think if he were alive today,'' or ''Wouldn't he be surprised to see all of this?'' People reflect on what their deceased spouses would do in certain situations, using memories of what the person would do as one of several options.

What is abnormal is the feeling that you must do things or see things just the way the deceased did. Sometimes in divorce, a spouse continues to allow the memory of a pressuring spouse to dominate his or her present life. This is unhealthy. This is continuing to maintain an emotional investment in the person. The phrase, "She would have wanted me to paint the house this color," could be indicative of continued emotional investment.

Sometimes when we lose something that has played a significant part in our lives, our memory of it becomes distorted. With the loss of a person, the usual response is to recall only the positive aspects. But in time, there must be realism. Thoughts and memories need to be reviewed realistically to include good and bad, positive and negative, situations we are glad occurred, and those we wish had not happened. By doing this, a balanced, realistic, accurate pool of memories develops. This is the image that is needed to develop the new relationship with the person. This realistic image will generate accompanying feelings as you face the realization that the person is no longer with you.[1]

At some point in time, it could be helpful to write a relationship history graph about the person you lost (especially a spouse through death or divorce) and identify the positives and negatives of your relationship. On page 84 is one such graph.

On the bottom portion of the graph, positive events and experiences are listed. It would be good to list five to fifteen separate events. The length of the vertical line indicates how much it meant to you. On the top part of the line, negative, upsetting, or hurtful experiences are identified. Again, the length of the vertical line indicates the intensity of the experience.

Upon completing this, you may find that other significant

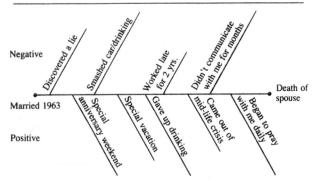

events come to mind. Add them. Now write a paragraph giving
as much description as possible for each event, both positive and
negative.

It is important to allow your feelings to emerge. Some of them
may come under the category of "regrets" or "if onlys." Take
the time to list all of the "if onlys" and "regrets." These could
pertain to both positive and negative experiences. Your list may
look something like this:

My feelings are all mixed up. I wish they were clearer.

I'll never forget the times we prayed together. They meant so
much.

I'm glad we have pictures and a video from our anniversaries.

I'm still hurt over the drinking. I wish it hadn't been a part of
our marriage.

I'm sorry for my angry outbursts.

I'm angry you died so young. I feel cheated. Our marriage was
getting better when you died. We needed more time.

I wish we could have talked more. There's so much more I
wanted to tell you.

Some of these statements may bring to mind such thoughts as,
I wish things could have been different, *I wish things had been*

better, *I wish we had spent* more *time together*, and *I* wonder *what would have happened if. . . .*

These statements reflect our own critical attitude toward what we did or didn't do and what the deceased person did or didn't do. If we remain in this critical stage, inaccurate memories of the relationship begin to emerge. The more this happens, the more difficult it is to complete our grief work.

If we are too critical of ourselves, we tend to overcompliment the person who is no longer there. Perhaps you have heard someone talk about a deceased partner as if the person were a saint:

"Oh, why didn't I appreciate him more. He was so. . . ."

"Oh, I'll never find such a sensitive person again."

"She was the perfect wife."

As you reflect on the "if onlys," "regrets," and what you wanted better, different, or more of, what do you discover about your relationship? What events still need to be resolved?

What you discover through this evaluation can bring you out of a pattern of denial and help you recover. Yes, it may seem the pain is too much and unnecessary, but it is very important and vital for developing this new relationship.[2]

What about recalling how a deceased person died? Is that necessary or normal? It is both. Repetitious reviewing helps you fully realize that your needs, hopes, expectations, and dreams of continuing to be with this person are not going to be fulfilled. You simply cannot be with this person the way you used to be, whether it is because of death or divorce. If the loss is by death, each time you review it and the surrounding events, your understanding of it will increase and perhaps more meaning will be added. You may tend to resist this since the memories bring pain, but each time you do it you discover you have a lot more control.[3]

Some people never seem to relinquish what they have lost. They hang on and dwell upon what they never had or what they lost, and it dominates their lives. Often, they become bitter. In the death of a child, some parents become involved in enshrinement. They keep their child alive by keeping his room just the way it was when he was alive. This can go on for many years. Unfortunately, this prolongs the grief.

Some respond with just the opposite reaction. After the loss occurs, whether it is the end of a love relationship, a death, a house that burned, or an unfulfilled job promotion, they act as though it never existed. They seem to block its existence from their memory and attempt to move on. Neither of these approaches reflects a healthy response. There needs to be a balance.

There are healthy ways to "hold on" to something you have lost. When you lose a parent, a spouse, a child, or even a very close friend, you don't want your life to be totally devoid of remembrance that the person once existed. It is important, not only for yourself but also to indicate to others that you have not forgotten that person. It is unreal and a form of denial to attempt to live life as though that person never existed or impacted your life. In healthy remembrance, you will find yourself having thoughts or doing, saying, and feeling things that show the other person continues to influence you.

But what are the healthy ways you can properly relate to a deceased loved one and keep the person alive for you and for others? This may sound strange, but the initial step is recognizing that the other person is gone and you are still alive. At first you may not feel as though you are very much alive. Sometimes people say they can't go on or don't want to go on without the one who left or died. But there does come that time of emotionally letting go and reinvesting in life in a new way.

Another step is deciding what there is about your life with the other person and your life together that can and should be retained. It means deciding what would be healthy. Do you continue to . . .

. . . go to the same coffee shop each morning for breakfast?

. . . go on an evening walk around the park?

. . . keep special items you either made or purchased together displayed?

. . . maintain any of the daily or weekly routines the two of you shared?

What do you purposely relinquish from your life with your partner? Attending the monthly couples Bible study and potluck dinner might not be retained, even if some encourage you to come back "once in a while." It could be too painful for some people, yet I have heard of others who continued in spite of the discomfort. Many of the couples activities, however, will be dropped.

Some healthy ways of relating to deceased people include . . .

. . . learning more about their favorite activities and involvements.

. . . looking at home movies or videos, listening to tapes of them, or reflecting on some of their stories to bring back memories of them.

. . . finally deciding to try some of their favorite foods or engage in their former activities, just to experience what they did.

Memories are preserved by visiting the deceased one's childhood school, job, and by going to the cemetery. Years after my father died, I was able to find his original homestead in Woolich, Maine, and even some distant relatives. This brought back memories and expanded my knowledge of my dad. It is perfectly all right and normal to talk about someone you lost, do things based on what you learned about the person, or reflect on memories. Part of who you are today and how you respond today is based upon your relationship with that person. Perhaps he or she taught you new insights, perceptions, skills, appreciations, or values, leaving an indelible mark upon you. Sometimes you may even be surprised as you discover yourself solving problems or responding in a manner the deceased used to do. This is often the case when you have lost a parent and years later resemble that parent in some way. You may exclaim, "Now, that's just the way Dad used to react!"

A real surprise for most people is the formation of a new identity. A student who has graduated from the security of four years at the same college and is plunged into the job market is no longer viewed by himself and others as a student. New roles, responsibilities, and expectations are now a part of his life. The way he views himself is changed. A young boy moving from the security of being an eighth-grader at his junior high school to a lowly freshman in a large high school means a new identity in the midst of his loss of familiar surroundings as well as status.

In the loss of a spouse, there is a change in identity from "we" to "I." This can be one of the most painful transitions of all. You see the world around you differently. Some of your friendships may change as well. You will retain old friendships, but adjustments have to be made. Your identity may have been as a couple and most of your friendships couple relationships. But now you are alone. Your time with couples will diminish. You will need both old and new relationships with people who share portions of your new identity with you.

No matter what you lost, it helps to be with and identify with others who have experienced the same loss as you, for they can assist you in the process of adjusting to your new identity.

A number of churches have developed support groups for all types of losses. One church even had a group for those with impaired vision and those who were going blind. Another church had a group for men who had lost their jobs and were seeking new directions vocationally. Parents who have lost a child through death, who have a handicapped child, a runaway, or a child on drugs benefit from being with others who have experienced the same loss. This new identity means learning new roles. Each change from the former identity needs to be named, faced, and grieved over.[4]

Recovery, as stated before, is reinvesting your emotional energy in something new that can give you satisfaction and fulfillment. The relationship with the person or object you lost cannot do this anymore. But I am not talking about a replacement. A new cat cannot replace the old one, a new dog cannot replace the dog you lost, a new person is not a replacement for a former love, and any attempt to make them replicas is an unhealthy response. Instead of replacing, you can reinvest in a service organization, ministry, a new career, a hope, and so on.

A major adjustment for anyone who has lost a loved one in death is what to do with the items left behind. This could involve tools, toys, clothes, specialty books, and other things. One way of handling this is the pile plan. The purpose is twofold: to take charge of the remaining items so they don't overwhelm you and to end up with what you really want to keep. It is often best to go through this procedure with another family member or close friend. Take all of the items and make three piles. In one pile are those items you are sure you want to keep. In the next one are those you are sure you want to dispose of. The third pile contains the things you are just not certain what to do with. Put away the items you want, give the others away, and place the uncertain items in boxes and keep them for a while until you are sure what you would like to do with them.

This is not an easy task. It is not without pain. But our lives go on, different and new. How different and new depends on our grief work.

Notes

Chapter 5 Adjusting to the Separation and Void

1. Therese A. Rando, *Grieving: How to Go On Living When Someone You Love Dies* (Lexington, Massachusetts: Lexington Books, 1988), 231–234, adapted.

2. John James and Frank Cherry, *The Grief Recovery Handbook* (New York: Harper and Row, Publishers, 1988), 109–121, adapted.

3. Rando, *Grieving*, 251, adapted.

4. Ibid., 238, 239, adapted.

6
Saying Good-bye

Retirement parties are normal occurrences. The retiree is honored and recognized for all the years of service. This get-together is also an opportunity for good-byes to be shared.

Over the years, we have had several receptionists and office personnel leave, and we usually have a farewell luncheon. It is an opportunity for those remaining not only to recognize the efforts of the person but also to officially bid the person good-bye. We probably won't see the person again, and we are recognizing this fact. When a friend leaves, relatives go home, or a good worker retires, there is a sadness in our good-byes. Every loss in life needs the recognition that the connection is broken and life will be different.

In death, the funeral service is a recognition that a person has left. It provides an opportunity for the mourners to say good-bye. I was twenty-two years old when I attended my first funeral. It was for my father, who had been killed in an automobile accident. I remember that one of his close friends walked by the casket, stopped, put his hand on it, and said, "Good-bye, Harry." This is quite common. For recovery to occur, we need to look back and say good-bye.

Sometimes mourners feel a lingering sadness because others failed to say good-bye in a proper way. Some of the events that contribute to incomplete feelings are . . .

. . . not enough friends or fellow workers respond with written expression, or they were unwilling to talk about the loss.

. . . the marker or plaque at the grave site either was delayed for months or was not appropriate.

. . . the person conducting the service failed to make the service meaningful because of lack of information.

. . . very few people came to pay their respects at the funeral home or at the actual service.

. . . there were no printed memorial service programs listing the person's dates of birth and death.

In other situations, similar problems can occur, delaying the completion of one's grief . . .

. . . a lack of recognition for the person retiring or leaving a job.

. . . a pet that ran away or was stolen, which afforded no opportunity to say good-bye.

. . . others downplaying the significance of a loss, making it difficult for the person to properly acknowledge it.

Being able to say good-bye helps us move toward closure and brings back some of the feelings of control over our life and circumstances that were diminished by the loss.[1]

When you say good-bye, you are acknowledging that you are no longer going to share your life with whatever you lost, whether it is a job, a place, a person, a dream, or even a part of your body. You will always have the memory, but now you acknowledge that you will live without whatever it was you lost.

What helps one person through grief may not be meaningful to others. Some parents who experience miscarriage simply move on with their lives and have no real need for good-byes. Others have a memorial service. Women who had abortions years ago often have memorial services as recognition of the deaths of their children.

In her book *Brainstorm,* Karen Brownstein describes her ordeal of brain surgery. Before the attendant shaved a portion of her head for the exploratory operation, Karen stood in front of the bathroom mirror, held and caressed her long hair, and said goodbye to it. Later, when she underwent radiation therapy for an inoperable, malignant tumor and subsequently lost all of her hair, it was easier for her to accept because she had held that brief good-bye ceremony.

Being able to anticipate a loss and how to cope with it makes it easier to handle. It is not uncommon to hear someone exclaim in anger, "He left, and I never got a chance to say good-bye to him."

Being able to say good-bye prior to the loss will help in the grieving process. Right after the doctor told us our son Matthew would probably die within the hour, we stood at his bedside and said good-bye to him. We said this in the midst of feelings of total helplessness. We wanted to stop the process of his dying, to reverse the decrease of his heartbeat, to open up his lungs to take in more air . . . but there was nothing to do but wait for him to die. And we said good-bye. We have said it more than once since he died. Often we say it when we find one of his personal items or even rediscover a memory.

I have talked to people who have driven to the location of a former place of employment, stood in front of the building, and said good-bye. Sometimes the farewell was out of a storehouse of positive memories, other times out of anger over the severing circumstances.

Is this a new thought for you? Who or what have you said good-bye to in your life? Is there something or someone you need to say good-bye to? No matter when the loss occurred, it is possible even now to say good-bye.

Years ago, I worked with a young man in counseling who had

lost his brother several years before. He had not returned to the
grave site since the funeral, and it was apparent that one of his
difficulties was not being able to fully grieve for his brother. One
day he went to the grave site and spent several hours there.
During that time, he said good-bye, and at last a chapter in his
life was closed.

Sometimes we engage in behavior that is a form of saying
good-bye, but we are not even aware of it. For several years, my
wife and I spent two or three weeks during the summer at an
antiquated ranch in the Grand Teton National Park. A delightful
older cowboy couple ran the ranch, and conditions were one step
shy of primitive. We had electric lights, but we hauled water
from a stream frequented by moose. We had many enjoyable
experiences there with our relatives and summer friends.

A few years ago, the ranch was sold to the park service. To
maintain a natural type of environment, it was closed down and
allowed to fall into a state of disrepair. Joyce and I went back for
a visit and looked through the ghost town, reflecting on our
experiences. Recently, when we drove to the ranch site to show
it to some friends, nothing was left. It looked as if the buildings
had never been there. As we drove off, we realized we probably
wouldn't return to that location again. There was no need. We
had our memories and we had said good-bye.

One of the better ways to say good-bye to many kinds of losses
is in writing. You might be surprised at the different kinds of
letters that have been written. The letter is both a way to say
good-bye and a way to express intense feelings of loss. It may be
an angry letter or one that is full of joy and sadness.

One person wrote to a friend who was about to die of cancer,
expressing his great appreciation for his friend.

Another person sent a good-bye letter to her elementary school
teacher, whom she had hoped would teach her own children but
who was now retiring.

A former addict wrote a farewell letter to his drugs, saying good-bye and describing what a problem they had been for him.

Many women have written good-bye letters to one of their breasts before or after a mastectomy. This has helped them with a loss that is very traumatic for a woman. It is a loss that is usually accompanied by an extended time of depression and mourning.

Over the years, numerous people have written letters to deceased friends, spouses, children, parents, brothers, sisters, or other significant people.[2] It helps to bring home the reality that a loved one is gone.

Good-bye letters are also appropriate during life's major transitions. I encourage parents who are about to see their daughter or son married to write the new son- or daughter-in-law a "welcome to the family" letter as well as a letter to their own son or daughter saying good-bye to him or her as an unmarried child. We did this when our daughter Sheryl was about to be married and sent it to her premarital counselor to give to her. It was addressed to our "about-to-be-married daughter" and was a letter of appreciation, encouragement, and good-bye to her previous position in life. (This letter is found in the final chapter of my book *Always Daddy's Girl*.) Her counselor, however, did not let her read the letter but had her bring it back home so I would have to read it aloud to her. And I did.

When Sheryl and Bill stepped down from the platform following the wedding ceremony, they handed to us and Bill's parents letters of thanks and appreciation for the past years. I would call letters like these transitional good-bye letters that also introduce new stages of life.

Saying good-bye is not morbid, pathological, or a sign of hysteria or being out of control. It is a healthy way to transition into the next phase of life.

How do you go about saying good-bye? First of all, identify what you think needs to be expressed in your good-bye. What are the actual words you want to say? What would express your appreciation and regrets or complete something that was never finished between the two of you?

Then write a good-bye letter or talk out loud to the person or whatever you have lost. If your letter is to a loved one who died, use the name you used most of the time in your life with this person.

You can address a good-bye letter to a lost dream, a lost hope, a business, or even a change in your vocational life. One divorced woman actually wrote a letter to her marriage and addressed it as though the loss were a real person. Indicate that it is a good-bye letter and then share what you want to say. The more regrets and ''if onlys'' you have, the more important your letter may be, since this is your opportunity to express what was never verbalized.

It helps to let your letter rest for a day and then read it out loud to yourself or to a trusted friend.

Recently a woman participant in my crisis counseling and grief recovery seminar wrote and shared with me the letters she had written to her deceased mother. This process took over fifteen months and included seventeen letters.

Following are the first letter she wrote to her mother, just a month after she died, and the final letter, fifteen months later.

                                                            January 1988

Dear Mom,

I must have started hundreds of letters like this over the years. Of course I can't write to you anymore, or call you. I've tried talking to you out loud, but even though I'm alone it feels strange. So I thought I'd write to you the way I did when you were alive. It's funny to talk about your life. Your life, as I know it and have experienced it, is over. I actually watched it leave you, inch by inch, those last weeks. It was agonizing to watch, because even though you were terribly sick you were always full of life.

The day you slipped into the coma I took something to

your closet before I left for home. As I stood there sur-
rounded by all those familiar clothes, I noticed the blue
flannel robe that Mamaw made you for Christmas a few
years back. Impulsively, I grabbed it and stuffed it into my
bag, almost feeling I was doing something wrong. I knew,
though, that this time you really weren't going to wear it
again, and somehow it seemed okay to take it. It smelled so
much like you that I slept with it that night. The next morning, when Holly called with the news, I ran to get it and
found that your fragrance was gone. And that, more than
the phone call, made me cry.

April 1989

Dear Mom,

It's been quite a while since I've written in this little
book. It's a gorgeous April day—brilliant blue skies, cool
breezes, and wildflowers bursting out all over the place.
Coming home from the nursery with a load of flowers this
morning, I was startled to see a young woman sobbing
openly behind the wheel of her car. Her face was so full of
pain that it seemed shocking in contrast to the bright, hope-
ful day around us. As I wondered what could be wrong, I
realized that the profound sense of grief that has permeated
my whole sense of being since you died WAS NOT
THERE. Much to the contrary, I was filled with the hope
and joy of the new spring day. My sorrow now feels less an
oppressive weight, more a . . . treasured possession. I can
take it out and ponder it, then put it safely and carefully
away. When I pass your portrait in the busy course of my
day, I pause and even smile before I rush on. Life is absolutely bursting with possibilities and challenges, and I'm so
excited about them all. Imagine that! And Mom, in the
middle of all this hope and excitement, I feel God here with
me. I feel joy.

All my love until we meet,

Jan

There are other ways to express good-byes. Sending a contribution to a church or charity in the name of the person can be an acknowledgment. Some people set up a living and lasting memorial through a scholarship, by donating a painting, planting a flower garden or a tree, or having a plaque made. At one of the large Christian conference grounds in Southern California, it is possible to dedicate a tree in the name of a loved one.

Have you ever shared with God how much you miss whatever you lost and shared with Him what you want to say in your good-byes?

June was a counselee who fought and resisted her divorce for years. Even five years later, she would not admit that she was a divorced woman. By not acknowledging her loss, she didn't properly grieve. As she worked through her feelings and the consequences of letting her ex-spouse continue to control her, she finally came to the place of writing him a very detailed and specific good-bye letter. In it, she said that she acknowledged and accepted her divorce and released her ex to do as he chose to do. She was going to move ahead with her life now that she was free. And at last she was.

In her descriptive and helpful book *Coming Back*, Ann Kaiser Stearns describes the death of her grandmother and how she said good-bye to her:

Honoring My "Granny"

When my grandmother died, I went back to the rural community of Thomas, Oklahoma, where I was born. The familiar billboard outside of town, near the skyscraper-sized grain elevator, greeted me once again with "1200 Friendly People Welcome You to Thomas."

The town was almost as I had left it many years before, except that the movie house and roller rink had closed and a storefront library had opened up on Main Street. Also the farmers, who still wore bib overalls, had exchanged their wide-brimmed hats for baseball caps with emblems advertising farm implements. Pickup trucks and an occasional car still parked diagonally on the street. People were still friendly and trusting. If you wanted to pay for something in a store, there was a stack of blank checkbooks on the counter by the cash register. You could fill out the check on one of the two banks in town. There was usually somebody around who knew you or one of your relatives, so there was no need for identification.

There were people here who still remembered my childhood visits to Granny and Grampa's house, remembered my mother with beautiful black hair in long braids, my father as a college student. Not many more years of life remained for most of these people, I sadly realized, and with them would pass away their treasure of memories.

I took a room at the local motel and drove my rental car to the funeral home. The purpose of my sentimental journey across the country was to reminisce, to pay tribute to the wonderful lady we called "Granny," and to mourn the approaching end of an era when the undertaker greeted you in a Western tie and black cowboy boots.

It pleased me that although I had the greatest distance to travel, I was the first family member to arrive at the funeral home. I wanted to be alone with my grandmother just one more time.

Entering the viewing room, I smiled at the pink casket. It would have pleased her, and it delighted me that somebody in the family had had the good sense to choose it. Closing the door behind me, I knew that I wanted to spend several hours with Granny. The flowers and prayer cards that had already come from my friends in Michigan and Maryland made it easier to be there.

"Granny," I said aloud, approaching her pretty casket, "I've always loved you and I always will." I stroked her cheeks, temples, and forehead with my young, tanned fingertips and patted her dear brown-spotted, wrinkled old hands. Finally my right hand rested on the knotted, arthritic joints of her fingers and the wide gold wedding band from a fifty-year marriage. She had been nearly ninety, and it struck me that I had never heard her complain about the arthritis that had so disfigured her hands.

"I'm so glad that you aren't suffering anymore," I went on, beginning to cry. "It hurt me so to see you these last years, locked up in your body, not remembering us, incontinent, and pitiful."

My grandmother had had only an eighth-grade education, yet she had read all of the Great Books, liked to sign her letters in Latin, and had published short stories and poems in farm magazines. At the age of sixty-nine, when she lived with me, she took courses in college, and we lived and traveled together in Europe for a year when she was seventy-five. At the nursing home where she had passed her last years and died, I once told the young employees what a proud, intelligent, personable, humorous, well-traveled, dignified lady she used to be. Older employees remembered Granny from another day: At the age of about eighty-four, when she was still in good health and of sound mind, she used to come regularly to the nursing home, as she put it, "to visit the old people."

I thanked Granny for faithfully remembering Christmas and my birthdays for as long as she was mentally capable and for sending all those twenty-five-dollar gift checks over the years. Once, after helping me finance a summer of study in the Middle East and giving my sister a piano, she had given each of her other grandchildren the equivalent in money, to be fair to them.

Remembering the one-dollar checks she liked to enclose in my letters made me smile and weep at the same time. Instructions were always written on the checks: "Treat" or "For Ice Cream." Never mind that I was thirty-four, still exchanging those checks for dollar bills: I loved it. The woman at the payroll window on the college campus where

I'm on the faculty always got a kick out of cashing Granny's checks, too.

After several hours with Granny at the funeral home, I left her side, saying, ''See you later, Granny, I'm going after a hamburger.'' I liked talking to her one last time in this routine way.

At the local fast food drive-in, a hallowed spot, I watched cowboys get in and out of their hay-loaded trucks and remembered countless meals and soft ice cream cones shared in a red Ford with Granny. The park where our family had had picnics and feasted on watermelon was in full view here too. Later at the florist I chose long-stemmed blue asters, one of my favorites, for Granny, and visited on the street with people who recognized me and offered condolences. A sentimental soul, I went to the old-fashioned local drugstore, where they still give you a milk shake in a metal cylinder. I must have tasted at least a hundred thousand chocolate milk shakes there with Granny over the years, and now I had one more in her honor along with a few more tears.

I drove out to spend some time parked near one of my grandparents' wheat fields and remembered the tornado that had taken the barn. I stopped by the cemetery and sat awhile by the ground that had already been broken for her grave. Grampa and Granny's gray marble tombstone was there, engraved with both names twenty years earlier. There had been visits with Granny to this place, I recalled, when we had brought flowers for Grampa. Leaving the cemetery, I drove back to town to retrace the streets where Granny had lived in various houses with my grandfather or alone, all the years of my life.

Determined that my remarkable and loving grandmother have the tribute she deserved, I returned to the motel to write the eulogy for her funeral service and a longer piece for Thomas's weekly newspaper. Later I saw to it that the minister knew the things about our Granny that we all cherished. It was important that he get acquainted with the person he was going to help us bury.

Our grandmother had traveled in a covered wagon across the Dakota and Nebraska territories, I told the minister. She had been orphaned, married young, and homesteaded with our grandfather in Oklahoma shortly after statehood. At her death, I said, she should be celebrated as a Pioneer Woman.

I remembered the mesmerizing stories Granny loved to tell of those turn-of-the-century days. The pioneer tales were so captivating that even late into my twenties I'd lie on her couch with my head cozily against a pillow on her lap. She would put her wrinkled hand on my shoulder and, like a young child, I would ask her to tell me about the long-ago days "just once more."

Now, with flowers in hand, I went to the nursing home to thank the staff there for taking care of my Granny, to ask about the circumstances of her final hours, to explain one more time why she was so dear to us all, and sadly to pack up her things. It pleased me to learn from one of the nurses that despite the ravages, indignities, and pitifulness of advanced Alzheimer's disease, a little piece of Granny's original, lively, spiritual self remained with her to the end. Her mind was gone to the point that she no longer recognized any of her relatives by name. A few days before her death, however, she was heard singing softly and tenderly from her bed. Clearly recognizable, the song she sang was "God Bless America."

Among Granny's modest belongings I found the beginnings of several letters written to me in the days when she still had partial memory but couldn't complete the tasks she began. Her letters were precious discoveries. I was especially glad that the envelopes were addressed to "Dr." because that meant she knew, before losing her mental faculties entirely, that I had finished the long-pursued education she had encouraged and aided.

It was a sweet goodbye that I had both with my Granny

and in her honor those two days in Thomas, Oklahoma. Years later I continue to hold cherished images in my mind of stroking her dear old wrinkled hands and telling her how much I loved her. The goodbyes that were said overlooking the family wheat field, by the homes where she lived, at the cemetery, the nursing home, the drugstore, the fast food drive-in, the funeral home, and elsewhere have made it possible for me to feel a sense of peace about my grandmother.

Granny had been dead for four years when my mother and I, on a trip together, decided to leave the interstate route and go out of our way a bit for a visit to the Thomas cemetery. On the narrow, slightly graveled road adjacent to my grandparents' tombstone, I parked the car facing the grave site. My mother and I sat awhile without speaking, holding hands. Eventually we got out of the car, spoke of Granny and of life and death in general, and moved about the marble marker, tidying up some dusty and faded artificial flowers. As we slowly walked back to our open car doors, I looked over my shoulder and said aloud something I'd almost forgotten. "Granny," I said with excitement, "I finally got a publisher for my first book!"

My mother, responding immediately, smiled warmly. "Oh, Ann," she said, "I think she already knows." We linked our arms and continued on toward the car.

I have felt Granny's loving presence at the milestone events of my life: buying a home, publishing my writings, becoming a mother. She is also present each day as someone whose love continues to warm, cheer, and encourage me. I feel she is whole again, no longer imprisoned by illness or frailty, and free to love us from where she is now.[3]

When Christians die, for us it is a matter of having to say good-bye, but for them it is a matter of being able to say hello to their Lord. This is why our feelings can sometimes be a mixture—

we are saddened for our loss but there is also a sense of joy for what the deceased person is now experiencing. We have a void in our lives, but the deceased person's life is now full and complete. The Christian death is a transition, a tunnel leading from this world into the next. There are many ways this transition can be depicted.

In the introduction to his book *The Secret of Staying in Love*, Father John Powell presents a beautiful description of this transition:

> This book is gratefully dedicated to Bernice. She has been a source of support in many of my previous attempts to write. She has generously contributed an excellent critical eye, a cultivated literary sense and especially a confident kind of encouragement. She did not help with the preparation of this book. On July 11 she received a better offer. She was called by the creator and the Lord of the Universe to join the celebration at the banquet of life.[4]

This was one way John Powell said good-bye to Bernice. As we grieve, the reality of our loss often overshadows the reality of where our loved one is. The emotions sweep over us like a flood drowning out the knowledge that in the future will become clearer and a source of strength for us. We need reminders of the meaning of death from the biblical perspective. For the Christian, death is a homegoing. David Morley describes the journey for us so beautifully:

> What a joyous moment that will be, when he will be re-united with all of his loved ones who have gone on before! When, once more, the lines of communication will be re-established, the old voices heard again, and the deathly silence at last broken forever—no more goodbyes, no more quick slipping away of loved ones into the mysterious enigma of death.

The most glorious anticipation of the Christian is that, at the time of death, he will come face-to-face with his blessed Lord, his wonderful, patient Redeemer, who all of those years continued to love him in spite of the countless times the man ignored Him and went his willful way. We will not be encountering a stranger, but the best and the most intimate friend that we have ever had. When we think of death as a time of revelation and reunion, we immediately remove its venom. We can say with the Apostle Paul, "Oh death, where is thy sting? Oh grave, where is thy victory?" (I Corinthians 15:15)[5]

A Christian is the one person who can have a different perspective on death. A Christian has a guarantee—not just of life here but forever. As one author said, "Death is ugly and it is repulsive, but it is not, I repeat, not able to bring the life of a Christian to a dreadful, screeching halt. God has worked out an alternate plan and it is a plan filled with soaring hope."

The hope of heaven with eternal life gives a greater meaning to this life. There is an old book called *God's Trombones* by James Weldon Johnson. Many people have read aloud his sermon "Go Down, Death" and found comfort from the honest struggle to portray the depths of our human sorrow.

Go Down, Death

Weep not, weep not,
She is not dead;
She's resting in the bosom of Jesus.
Heart-broken husband—weep no more;
Grief-stricken son—weep no more;
Left-lonesome daughter—weep no more;
She's only just gone home.

Day before yesterday morning,
God was looking down from his great, high heaven,
Looking down on all his children,

And his eye fell on Sister Caroline,
Tossing on her bed of pain.
And God's big heart was touched with pity,
With the everlasting pity.

And God sat back on his throne,
And he commanded that tall, bright angel standing at his right hand:
Call me Death!
And that tall, bright angel cried in a voice
That broke like a clap of thunder:
Call Death!—Call Death!
And the echo sounded down the streets of heaven
Till it reached away back to that shadowy place,
Where Death waits with his pale, white horses.

And Death heard the summons,
And he leaped on his fastest horse,
Pale as a sheet in the moonlight.
Up the golden street Death galloped,
And the hoofs of his horse struck fire from the gold,
But they didn't make no sound.
Up Death rode to the Great White Throne,
And waited for God's command.

And God said: Go down, Death, go down,
Go down to Savannah, Georgia,
Down in Yamacraw,
And find Sister Caroline.
She's borne the burden and heat of the day,
She's labored long in my vineyard,
And she's tired—
She's weary—
Go down, Death, and bring her to me.

And Death didn't say a word,
But he loosed the reins of his pale, white horse,
And he clamped the spurs to his bloodless sides,
And out and down he rode,

Through heaven's pearly gates,
Past suns and moons and stars;
On Death rode,
And the foam from his horse was like a comet in the sky;
On Death rode,
Leaving the lightning's flash behind;
Straight on down he came.
While we were watching round her bed,
She turned her eyes and looked away,
She saw what we couldn't see;
She saw Old Death. She saw Old Death,
Coming like a falling star.
But Death didn't frighten Sister Caroline;
He looked to her like a welcome friend.
And she whispered to us: I'm going home,
And she smiled and closed her eyes.

And Death took her up like a baby,
And she lay in his icy arms,
But she didn't feel no chill.
And Death began to ride again—
Up beyond the evening star,
Out beyond the morning star,
Into the glittering light of glory,
Onto the Great White Throne.
And there he laid Sister Caroline
On the loving breast of Jesus.

And Jesus took his own hand and wiped away her tears,
And he smoothed the furrows from her face,
And the angels sang a little song,
And Jesus rocked her in his arms,
And kept a-saying: Take your rest,
Take your rest, take your rest.

Weep not—weep not,
She is not dead;
She's resting in the bosom of Jesus.

In Max Lucado's inspirational book *The Applause of Heaven*, he concludes with a chapter on going home. He begins the chapter by describing his conclusion to a long trip and finally arriving at the airport. His wife and three daughters are excited that he is home. But one of them has a very interesting response. In the midst of the shouts of joy that he is home, she stops long enough to clap. She applauds for him. Isn't that different? But isn't it affirming and appropriate! Then he proceeds to talk about the Christian's ultimate home and homegoing. Surely Jesus, too, will clap when we arrive home.

In Revelation 21:1–5 NIV, we read John's description of what our homegoing will be like:

> Then I saw a new heaven and a new earth, for the first heaven and the first earth had passed away, and there was no longer any sea. I saw the Holy City, the new Jerusalem, coming down out of heaven from God, prepared as a bride beautifully dressed for her husband. And I heard a loud voice from the throne saying, ''Now the dwelling of God is with men, and he will live with them. They will be his people, and God himself will be with them and be their God. He will wipe every tear from their eyes. There will be no more death or mourning or crying or pain, for the old order of things has passed away.

> John says that someday God will wipe away your tears. The same hands that stretched the heavens will touch your cheeks. The same hands that formed the mountains will caress your face. The same hands that curled in agony as the Roman spike cut through will someday cup your face and brush away your tears forever.

> When you think of a world where there will be no reason to cry, ever, doesn't it make you want to go home?

> ''There will be no more death . . .'' John declares. Can you imagine it? A world with no hearses or morgues or

cemeteries or tombstones? Can you imagine a world with no
spades of dirt thrown on caskets? No names chiseled into
marble? No funerals? No black dresses? No black wreaths?

In the next world, John says, "good-bye" will never be
spoken.[6]

Every person on earth is appointed to die at some time. We
fear it, resist it, try to postpone it, and even deny its existence.
But it won't work. We cannot keep our loved ones from dying.
We cannot keep ourselves from dying. But we can see it from
God's perspective. Max Lucado concludes his book with what
homegoing means from a new perspective:

> Before you know it, your appointed arrival time will come;
> you'll descend the ramp and enter the City. You'll see faces
> that are waiting for you. You'll hear your name spoken by
> those you love. And, maybe, just maybe—in the back,
> behind the crowds—the One who would rather die than live
> without you will remove his pierced hands from his heav-
> enly robe and . . . *applaud.*[7]

Yes, your loved ones who died are saying hello. You have said
good-bye to them. Soon you will be saying hello to a new day
without them . . . for now!

Notes

Chapter 6 Saying Good-bye

1. Ann Kaiser Stearns, *Coming Back* (New York: Ballantine Books,
   1988), 104, 105, adapted.

2. Ibid., 110–112, adapted.

3. Ibid., 126–130.

4. John Powell, S. J., *The Secret of Staying in Love* (Niles, Illinois: Argus Publications, 1974), dedication.

5. David C. Morley, *Halfway Up the Mountain* (Old Tappan, New Jersey: Fleming H. Revell Company, 1979), 77, 78.

6. Max Lucado, *The Applause of Heaven* (Dallas, Texas: WORD Incorporated, 1990), 186, 187.

7. Ibid., 190.

7

Recovering From Loss

"How will I know? What will be the indication when it's over? How will I feel when I've recovered from my loss?"

Have you ever asked these common questions? We want to know both when it will happen and how we will know. Recovery is essential for any kind of loss, but the actual recovery period will vary, depending upon the type of loss and its intensity. Think back to the most recent loss in your life. Where are you in the recovery process? If you feel you have recovered, how did you know when it happened?

Have you ever been in the hospital for an operation? If so, you know the procedure. After the operation is over, you are taken to a recovery room, where you stay for a few hours until the effects of the anesthetic begin to wear off. The term *recovery* is a bit misleading for this room. It certainly doesn't mean total recovery. It means helping you adjust to the effects of the operation so you are ready for the real recovery, which will take time.

Ann Kaiser Stearns describes the process of recovery in the early stages of grief:

Recovery from loss is like having to get off the main highway every so many miles because the direct route is under reconstruction. The road signs reroute you through little towns you hadn't expected to visit and over bumpy roads you hadn't wanted to bounce around on. You are basically traveling in the appropriate direction. On the map, however, the course you are following has the look of shark's teeth instead of a straight line. Although you are gradually getting there, you sometimes doubt that you will ever meet up with the finished highway.[1]

In some ways, this is similar to recovery from loss. Recovery does not mean a once-and-for-all conclusion to your loss and grief. It is a twofold process involving regaining your ability to function as you once did and resolving and integrating your loss into your life. But, yes, there is something else to recovery. In a sense, you will never recover completely because you will never be exactly the way you were before. Your loss changes you. As someone once asked in a counseling session, "If I can't be the way I was before and I never recover completely, what is all this about recovery? I'm confused. What does it mean? How can you recover and not fully recover?"

Recovery means you get your capabilities and attributes back so you can use them. Part of the process means you are no longer fighting your loss but accepting it. Acceptance doesn't mean you would have chosen it or even that you like it. You have learned to live with it as a part of your life. Recovery doesn't mean you don't mourn occasionally. It means you learn to live with your loss so you can go on with your life.

I still have a scar from an incision made during an operation when I was a child. In a sense, it serves as a reminder to me that I had that experience. Recovery is like a scar from an operation, but it is in such a sensitive place that on occasion you feel the ache again. You cannot predict when it will happen.

Recovery means reinvesting in life, looking for new relationships and new dreams. A newfound source of joy is possible. But you could very well feel uncomfortable with whatever is new. You may feel that to experience the joys of life again is somehow wrong. Besides, if you begin to hope or trust again, you could experience another loss.

Remember the source of our joy. It is the Lord. The Psalmist states that He "clothes us with joy." God is the One who extends to you the invitation to reinvest in life.

If you have experienced a recent loss, ask yourself these questions: What might be making it difficult for me to reinvest in life at this time? What would help me to reinvest in life?[2]

> I will exalt you, O Lord,
>> for you lifted me out of the depths
>> and did not let my enemies gloat over me.
> O Lord my God, I called to you for help
>> and you healed me.
> O Lord, you brought me up from the grave;
>> you spared me from going down into the pit.
> Sing to the Lord, you saints of his;
>> praise his holy name.
> For his anger lasts only a moment,
>> but his favor lasts a lifetime;
> weeping may remain for a night,
>> but rejoicing comes in the morning.
> When I felt secure, I said,
>> "I will never be shaken."
> O Lord, when you favored me,
>> you made my mountain stand firm;
> but when you hid your face,
>> I was dismayed.
> To you, O Lord, I called;
>> to the Lord I cried for mercy:

"What gain is there in my destruction,
   in my going down into the pit?
Will the dust praise you?
   Will it proclaim your faithfulness?
Hear, O Lord, and be merciful to me;
   O Lord, be my help."
You turned my wailing into dancing;
   you removed my sackcloth and clothed me with joy,
that my heart may sing to you and not be silent.
   O Lord my God, I will give you thanks forever.

                                         Psalm 30 NIV

Did you notice what was said in this psalm about grief and recovery?

In grief we sometimes feel as if we are going to die. Have you felt that way?

In grief we sometimes feel as if God has hidden His face. Have you felt that way?

In grief we also have times when we feel God has favored us. Have you felt that way?

In recovery we discover that weeping will not last forever. Are there clothes of mourning that you would like to exchange for clothes of joy?

Do you also realize that you have a choice in your recovery? Most people do not have a choice in their loss, but everyone has a choice in their recovery. The changes in your identity, relationships, new roles, and even abilities can be either positive or negative. This is where you have a choice.

I have seen people who choose to live in denial and move ahead as though nothing has really happened. I have seen those stuck in the early stages of their grief who choose to live a life of bitterness and blame. Some become so hardened and angry that it is difficult to be around them for an extended period of time. They have made a choice. It is not the fault of other people or of

God. Since life is full of losses, we have the choice of doing something constructive or destructive with our loss.

Is there any kind of criteria a person can use at some point in the process of grieving to evaluate whether or not recovery is occurring? Yes, there is. However, it often helps to go through this evaluation with a person who can assist you with an objective viewpoint. Dr. Therese Rando[3] has made an outstanding contribution to the study of grief and recovery. She suggests that recovery should be seen by observing changes in yourself, in your relationship with what you lost, and in your relationship with the world and other people in it. As you read the following evaluation, the conclusions you reach may help you to decide where you are in your recovery. On a scale of 0–10 (0 meaning "not at all" and 10 meaning "total recovery in that area"), rate yourself in response to each question. This evaluation is geared toward the loss of a person, but it can be adapted to other losses as well.

Changes in Myself Because of My Loss

I have returned to my normal levels of functioning in most areas of my life.

0 ----------------------------5 ----------------------------10

My overall symptoms of grief have declined.

0 ----------------------------5 ----------------------------10

My feelings do not overwhelm me when I think about my loss or when someone mentions it.

0 ----------------------------5 ----------------------------10

Most of the time I feel all right about myself.

0 ----------------------------5 ----------------------------10

I enjoy myself and what I experience without feeling guilty.

0 ----------------------------5 ----------------------------10

My anger has diminished, and when it occurs, it is handled appropriately.

0 ---------------------------5 ---------------------------10

I don't avoid thinking about things that could be or are painful.

0 ---------------------------5 ---------------------------10

My hurt has diminished and I understand it.

0 ---------------------------5 ---------------------------10

I can think of positive things.

0 ---------------------------5 ---------------------------10

I have completed what I need to do about my loss.

0 ---------------------------5 ---------------------------10

My pain does not dominate my thought or my life.

0 ---------------------------5 ---------------------------10

I can handle special days or dates without being totally over-whelmed by memories.

0 ---------------------------5 ---------------------------10

I have handled the secondary losses that accompanied my major loss.

0 ---------------------------5 ---------------------------10

I can remember the loss on occasion without pain and without crying.

0 ---------------------------5 ---------------------------10

There is meaning and significance to my life.

0 ---------------------------5 ---------------------------10

I am able to ask the question How? rather than Why? at this time.

0 ---------------------------5 ---------------------------10

I see hope and purpose in life, in spite of my loss.

0 ---------------------------5 ---------------------------10

I have energy and can feel relaxed during the day.

0 ---------------------------5 ---------------------------10

I no longer fight the fact that the loss has occurred. I have accepted it.

0 ---------------------------5 ---------------------------10

I am learning to be comfortable with my new identity and in being without what I lost.

0 ---------------------------5 ---------------------------10

I understand that my feelings over the loss will return periodically, and I can understand and accept that.

0 ---------------------------5 ---------------------------10

I understand what grief means and have a greater appreciation for it.

0 ---------------------------5 ---------------------------10

Changes in My Relationship With the Person I Lost

I remember our relationship realistically with positive and negative memories.

0 ---------------------------5 ---------------------------10

The relationship I have with the person I lost is healthy and appropriate.

0 ---------------------------5 ---------------------------10

I feel all right about not thinking about the loss for a time. I am not betraying the one I lost.

0 ---------------------------5 ---------------------------10

I have a new relationship with the person I have ''lost.'' I know appropriate ways of keeping the person ''alive.''

0 ---------------------------5 ---------------------------10

I no longer go on a search for my loved one.
0 ---------------------------------5 ---------------------------------10

I don't feel compelled to hang on to the pain.
0 ---------------------------------5 ---------------------------------10

The ways I keep my loved one alive are healthy and acceptable.
0 ---------------------------------5 ---------------------------------10

I can think about things in life other than what I lost.
0 ---------------------------------5 ---------------------------------10

My life has meaning even though this person is gone.
0 ---------------------------------5 ---------------------------------10

Changes I Have Made in Adjusting to My New World

I have integrated my loss into my world and I can relate to others
in a healthy way.
0 ---------------------------------5 ---------------------------------10

I can accept the help and support of other people.
0 ---------------------------------5 ---------------------------------10

I am open about my feelings in other relationships.
0 ---------------------------------5 ---------------------------------10

I feel it is all right for life to go on even though my loved one is
gone.
0 ---------------------------------5 ---------------------------------10

I have developed an interest in people and things outside myself
that have no relationship to the person I lost.
0---------------------------------5---------------------------------10

I have put the loss in perspective.
0---------------------------------5---------------------------------10[4]

Grief recovery is a back-and-forth process. One of the better ways to identify your progress is through a personal journal. This will give you the proof that you are making progress even though your feelings say otherwise. Your journal is your own private property and is not for anyone else to read. It is an expression of what you are feeling and your recovery climb. It can be written in any style. It can be simple statements, poems, or prayers that reflect your journey. The authors of the *Grief Adjustment Guide* offer some helpful suggestions for a journal.

1. You may find it helpful to make time every day to write at least a short paragraph in your journal. At the end of a week, review what you have written to see small steps of progress toward grief recovery. Writing at least a line or two every day is the most effective way to keep a journal.

2. Some people write in their journals a few times each week, reviewing them at the end of the week and at the end of each month.

If you have trouble getting started, look over the following list of suggested beginnings. Find one that fits what you are feeling or need to express and use it to ''jump start'' your writing for that day:

1. My biggest struggle right now is . . .
2. The thing that really gets me down is . . .
3. The worst thing about my loss is . . .
4. When I feel lonely . . .
5. The thing I most fear is . . .
6. The most important thing I've learned is . . .
7. The thing that keeps me from moving on is . . .
8. I seem to cry most when . . .
9. I dreamed last night . . .
10. I heard a song that reminded me of . . .
11. A new person I've come to appreciate is . . .
12. I get angry when . . .
13. Part of the past that keeps haunting me is . . .
14. What I've learned from the past is . . .

15. Guilt feelings seem to come most when . . .

16. The experiences I miss the most are . . .

17. New experiences I enjoy the most are . . .

18. The changes I least and most like are . . .

19. My feelings sometimes confuse me because . . .

20. I smelled or saw something today that reminded me of . . .

21. A new hope I found today is . . .

22. New strengths I've developed since my loss are . . .

23. I feel close to God today because . . .

24. I am angry at God today because . . .

25. For me to find and have balance, I . . .

26. I got a call or letter from a friend today that . . .

27. My friend, _____, had a loss today, and I . . .[5]

If one of these doesn't fit, then write about what you *are* feeling. You could start with just one word—*misery, longing, hope,* or whatever—and then describe that feeling with phrases or sentences. If you need to, cry as you write, but keep writing until there is nothing more to say about that feeling.

Your journal is yours to say and feel what is in your heart and mind. It is your way of crystallizing the feelings of loss. Dealing with your feelings one at a time in a written, tangible form is a good way to "own" those feelings and respond to them in an organized way. Grief is a whole tangle of feelings, and writing them down is a great way to isolate and adjust to each one.

Monitor what you write. When you begin to see yourself writing more about what is happening *today* and less about the one you have lost, you'll know that healing and adjustment are indeed taking place, though it may seem painfully slow. Look for signs of progress.

It is *your* journal; use it for your own benefit.[6]

Perhaps the chart on page 121 will assist you in your journey of recovery. Use it with the accompanying evaluation questions.

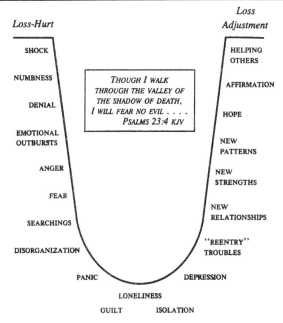

Loss
Adjustment

Loss-Hurt

SHOCK

NUMBNESS

DENIAL

EMOTIONAL
OUTBURSTS

ANGER

FEAR

SEARCHINGS

DISORGANIZATION

PANIC

LONELINESS

GUILT   ISOLATION

HELPING
OTHERS

AFFIRMATION

HOPE

NEW
PATTERNS

NEW
STRENGTHS

NEW
RELATIONSHIPS

"REENTRY"
TROUBLES

DEPRESSION

*THOUGH I WALK
THROUGH THE VALLEY OF
THE SHADOW OF DEATH,
I WILL FEAR NO EVIL . . . .
PSALMS 23:4 KJV*

1. Cross out the stages you have already experienced.
2. List ways you have freed yourself from being "stuck" in one phase.
3. Make some statements to yourself about your own patterns of handling loss experiences. (Examples: "I turn inward instead of outward." "I internalize my anger.")
4. List the strengths you now have because of the grief you have experienced. (Examples: "I'm a survivor!" "I've learned empathy for others.")
5. What are ways you can use these new strengths to help others?[7]

Notes

Chapter 7 Recovering From Loss

1. Ann Kaiser Stearns, *Living Through Personal Crisis* (Chicago: Thomas More Press, 1984), 85, 86.

2. Dale and Juanita Ryan, *Recovery From Loss* (Downers Grove, Illinois: InterVarsity Press, 1990), 40, 41, adapted.

3. Therese A. Rando, *Grieving: How to Go On Living When Someone You Love Dies* (Lexington, Massachusetts: Lexington Books, 1988), 281–283, adapted.

4. Ibid., 284–286, adapted.

5. Charlotte Greeson, Mary Hollingsworth, and Michael Washburn, *The Grief Adjustment Guide* (Sisters, Oregon: Questar Publishers, Inc., 1990), 90, 91.

6. Ibid.

7. Ibid., 68.

8

Growing Through Our Losses

Four men from a Central American country were adrift in their small fishing boat for months. *Reader's Digest* carried a story about their experiences. The focus of the story was on how they survived.

A plane crashes and isn't found for ten days. Fourteen people are still alive. The question asked is, "How did you stay alive?"

A car crashes through a guardrail on a deserted mountain road and three injured people are found alive five days later. The question asked of each of them is, "How did you survive that ordeal?"

This is the same question to consider when we experience a major loss, for recovery has to do with being a survivor. Some people resolve their crisis and survive. But some don't. What makes the difference? Are there some principles that could help each of us face a loss?

First, let's define a survivor. I like psychiatrist Joy Joffe's definition: "A survivor is a person who, when knocked down, somehow knows to stay down until the count of nine and then to get up differently. The nonsurvivor gets up right away and gets hit again."[1]

1. Survivors plan ahead, if at all possible, so they can be prepared for a transition, loss, or a crisis. Survivors have found a way to cope with and master what they experience.

Life is full of predictable transitions that have the potential to become major losses unless the question, "How can I best prepare for this and what will it mean to me?" is answered. Consider some of the typical transitions.

Both men and women go through identity adjustments at fairly predictable stages of life. Those who have children will experience the empty nest. For some couples, the empty nest is a major loss and adjustment. Their sense of loss and change is very intense. The atmosphere of the home changes, and secondary losses are confronted as well. There are fewer choices to make, less confusion and noise. Old habit patterns of shopping, cooking, scheduling—use of time—will change. New roles have to be established and new pressures may result. Needs formerly filled by children will be directed to someone else for fulfillment. These needs include communication, affection, and companionship. Frequently, the upheaval of children preparing to leave home hits at the same time as the mid-life transition or even mid-life crisis. Many studies show that when the last child leaves home, there is an increased likelihood of marital maladjustment. If that is the case, this problem with all of its ramifications can be anticipated and handled in advance.

Retirement is a major loss for many people, yet very few anticipate and plan for this event.

Physical changes or deterioration can be handled well in advance. An individual who has ALS (Lou Gehrig's disease) shared with me that he had taken several steps in terms of adjusting his work habits, the type of car he traveled in, the layout of his home, and the financial life-style of his family, so that the next few years would be easier for his wife and him to handle.

Another man, who had multiple sclerosis, changed professions at the early stage of the disease so he could continue working for a number of years in a job he could handle.

These are people who took charge of the potential loss in advance and were able to continue with life. Even learning about grief and its characteristics in advance can be a help as you go through the process. Reflect: In what way have you anticipated changes or losses in your life?

2. Survivors have learned from the wisdom and experience of others. They often do this even before they experience a loss but are also eager to learn during the experience itself. They don't try to carry the load themselves but look to others for insights they lack. Reflect: How do you handle loss in your life? Who helps you?

3. Survivors are not complainers. They handle their feelings well and, even though there may be periodic bouts with feeling sorry for themselves, they don't whine, grumble, complain, or become bitter. They seem to have discovered the futility of this attitude earlier in their lives. Reflect: What do you hear yourself saying when difficulties confront you?

4. Survivors have role models. These role models inspire them through the way they handle adversity in their own lives. Survivors observe what their role models did, how they did it, and look carefully at the underlying attitudes. When you see what is possible in others, that in itself can give you hope. Reflect: Who are the role models in your life?

5. Survivors have a desire to continue to learn and grow. It means stretching mind and attitude to look at something in a new way. It means being willing to branch out and learn something even if you are quite comfortable with what you are doing at this time. Reflect: In what way have you grown and changed over the past year?

6. Survivors do not blame. This is a very easy trap to fall into. Often blame stems from our own feelings of guilt or personal responsibility, even though we were not responsible. If a child dies in a car accident, the parents may blame one another, the manufacturer of the car, the doctors, the medics, or God. In some cases, other people may in fact be responsible, but to fasten our feelings on that issue will keep us stuck in our grief. So much blame is uncalled for and has little basis in reality. Reflect: Evaluate the tendency in your life to blame others for your losses.

"All of us feel powerless at times," Ann Kaiser Stearns says, "because we are human beings. Triumphant survivors, however, trade in the position of helplessness for a decision to take charge and search for options."[2]

7. *When a major crisis or loss occurs, survivors are able to develop a way to cope with the loss.* They identify the problems and learn to respond as if they are in control. They don't give up on themselves or on life. They come to the place where they are able to say, "Let's see what can be done to survive."

It took over four years to turn around one of my businesses so that financially it was in the black instead of losing money. Part of the turnaround was painful, for it meant changing some business relationships with friends and cutting back. But it was a wise decision. Reflect: How well are you able to identify coping skills and new ways of handling major problems?

8. *Survivors find a way to live in spite of what has happened to them.* They find some way to excel in an area or to express themselves. I remember listening one Sunday to the offertory at church being played by a concert pianist. He had been born blind and partially deaf. I am amazed when I watch Jim Abbott pitch for the California Angels baseball team. He has only one good hand and arm, yet he has overcome that loss. It took years, but he never gave up. Determination is a necessary trait to survive. Reflect: How have you discovered new ways to move ahead in your life when adversity hits?

9. *Even in the midst of grief, survivors can still enjoy life and laugh at times.* Yes, it is possible to laugh even when we are hurting. Sometimes we laugh at something a deceased person

said or did when alive. Often after a funeral, there is laughter as people visit with one another. Reflect: Are you able to enjoy life even when it seems to be crumbling around you?

10. Survivors have the ability to be flexible and adapt to new situations. They are able to discover strength through adversity. They are able to come up with a variety of ways to respond to what has happened. They don't persist in living just one way but are able to adapt. Survivors do not always respond to situations the same way.[3] Reflect: What is your source of strength that enables you to grow and move ahead?

11. Survivors have faith in God. Having faith in Jesus Christ and developing a biblical perspective on life is the foundation for survival and recovery. Correct theology also helps us accept what happens in life. I don't mean that we always understand it or like it, but we do learn to accept it. Do you understand a cancer ward filled with children under the age of ten? Or the young mother of three run down by a drunken driver? What about the businessman who was honest and followed biblical teachings in his company, yet it failed?

Some Christians live by assumptions that are not biblically based. For example:

Life is fair.

I can control what happens to me.

If I follow Christ and His teachings, no tragedy will happen to me.

If I am suffering, it is because I am sinning.

My body was meant to live forever . . . at least until age ninety!

If I tithe, God will bless me financially.

It is so important to deal with the questions and issues of life before the deep hurts of life confront us. When we don't, too often God gets the blame.

Some people need to find a guilty party for their loss, and if they can't find one, they invent one. Sometimes we look at tragedies, shrug our shoulders, and say it is the will of God. When Mount St. Helens erupted, the Cowlitz Indians believed it came from the anger of God over the desecration of their burial grounds. After the massive earthquake in Mexico City in 1985, some people said, "God must be angry."

In her excellent book *Helping People Through Grief*, Delores Kuenning writes that we cannot

> suddenly draw from deep reservoirs of faith within ourselves if nothing has been done to nurture our spiritual lives in the past. . . . As human beings made of flesh and blood and bone rather than rubber, steel, or plastic, our reasoning tells us that generally deaths are caused by: errors in human judgment or planning; diseases (some of which are self-imposed); genetic disorders; the evil action of others; violence against self; acts of nature such as earthquake, wind, fire, and flood; and unbending natural laws such as the force of gravity.
>
> Our reasoning also tells us that when we violate the God-given commandments—which are really positive statements designed to help us live a healthy, uncomplicated life—we create the conditions that can wreak havoc with our personal lives. When we disobey God's laws of health, for example, we can expect sickness and the suffering that goes with it. Our bodies are designed by God and require healthful living habits to function properly.[4]

Dr. Dwight Carlson, a Christian psychiatrist, writes:

> The belief that God is in control of the universe leads some people to conclude He has planned every last detail and wants every event to come about exactly as it does. Such a God would delight in pushing misfortune buttons: this God says, "Let's give Mary an 'A' on her English test today. Let's give Joanne a dent in her fender. I'll clog up

Pat's sink. Joe will get a heart attack, and I'll give Susan leukemia." Nothing could be further from the truth.[5]

The other side of blaming God is believing that we are special because of our relationship with Him or because we have done something for Him, and therefore He will insulate us from the misfortunes of life. "God might intervene—at his sovereign choosing—but it is not our divine right to demand his intervention."[6]

Pain—death—tragedy—suffering. When they hit us we feel tormented, and the age-old questions emerge: Why does God allow suffering? Where is He in our suffering? Does it have any meaning?

> We all fear pain; yet from infancy it serves as a warning mechanism within our bodies to protect us from the hot stove or alert us to an inflammatory process within. But when it ravages our bodies, or the body of a loved one, it sears the soul and torments us physically, emotionally, and spiritually. *Why does God allow suffering?* we ask. *Does suffering have meaning?*
>
> Daniel Simundson, in *Where Is God in My Suffering?* reminds us that "when we cry out to God in our times of suffering, we know that we will be heard by one who truly knows what we have gone through. It is a great comfort for a sufferer to know the presence of an understanding and compassionate God, who not only invites our very human prayers but also knows what it is like to be in so much pain. God hears. God understands. God suffers with us. The lament is heard by One who has been there.[7]

The Source for what we believe has to be the Word of God. When we look at it, we discover that time and time again it states God is good and He has a concern for mankind. We also know that God is omnipotent. That means He is all-powerful. But what does *all-powerful* mean to you? Sometimes we attribute incorrect meanings to it. Does *all-powerful* mean we are robots and He causes every single thing that happens in the world? He is all-powerful, but that doesn't necessarily mean everything that happens in the world is the way He wants it. At the creation of the world, He created mankind with choice. Because of the choices of man, there are results that are not what God desires. God could not give us the freedom to love Him if we didn't have the freedom to reject Him and His teachings. He wants us to love Him based upon our own choice.

Dr. Dwight Carlson writes:

> It is further possible that since God greatly desires individuals who willingly love, worship, and follow Him, He had no alternative but to allow Satan to test them with pain, suffering, and misfortune. This is one of the major points taught in the Book of Job. Let me assure you that this does *not* mean God is not sovereign; in the Book of Job, Satan had to request permission to test Job, and God allowed it only within very fixed limits (Job 2:6).
>
> Recognition of God's self-imposed limitations is the most difficult concept to grasp in this book. Many ardent Christians will have difficulty with this viewpoint. But I am convinced that when God created the world, He set laws in motion which even He chooses to honor. The problem for us is that these laws intersect our lives in the most sensitive areas—in our suffering and misfortune.[8]

This leads to an interesting question: Who is at the center of the universe—God or us? In his book *When Bad Things Happen to Good People*, Harold Kushner asks:

> If God can't make my sickness go away, what good is He? Who needs Him? God does not want you to be sick or crippled. He didn't make you have this problem, and He

doesn't want you to go on having it, but He can't make it go
away. That is something which is too hard even for God.
What good is He, then?[9]

This question raised by Kushner seems to reflect the thought
that we are at the center of the universe and God is there to do our
bidding. But C. S. Lewis has a different perspective: "Man is not
the center. God does not exist for the sake of man. Man does not
exist for his own sake."[10]

John Killinger shares an interesting thought concerning how
we handle the difficulties of life and how we worship:

> Somehow, joy arises from loss and suffering and toil as
> much as it does from pleasure and ease. It is much deeper
> than the surface of existence; it has to do with the whole
> structure of life. It is the perfume of the rose that is crushed,
> the flash of color in the bird that is hit, the lump in the throat
> of the man who sees and knows, instinctively, that life is a
> many splendored thing.
>
> Don't misunderstand me. I am not suggesting that God
> sends adversity to enhance our appreciation of life or to
> make us more aware of His nearness. Nor am I implying
> that the fullness of life comes only to those who have passed
> through deep waters. Rather, I am saying that God is present
> in all of life, including its tragedies. His presence trans-
> forms even these agonizing experiences into opportunities
> for worship.
>
> In one day, Job lost everything—his servants, his live-
> stock, his wealth and his children. "At this, Job got up and
> tore his robe and shaved his head. Then he fell to the ground
> in worship and said: 'Naked I came from my mother's
> womb, and naked I will depart. The Lord gave and the Lord
> has taken away; may the name of the Lord be praised.' In all
> this Job did not sin by charging God with wrongdoing"
> (Job 1:20–22).[11]

Richard Exley continues this thought:

> We don't worship God because of our losses, but in spite of them. We don't praise Him for the tragedies, but in them. Like Job, we hear God speak to us out of the storm (Job 38:1). Like the disciples at sea in a small boat, caught in a severe storm, we too see Jesus coming to us in the fourth watch of the night. We hear Him say, "Take courage! It is I. Don't be afraid" (Matthew 14:27). . . .
>
> If you've lived for any length of time, you've probably had opportunity to see the different ways people respond to adversity. The same tragedy can make one person better and another person bitter. What makes the difference? Resources. Inner resources developed across a lifetime through spiritual disciplines. *If you haven't worshipped regularly in the sunshine of your life, you probably won't be able to worship in the darkness.* If you haven't been intimate with God in life's ordinariness, it's not likely that you will know how or where to find Him should life hand you some real hardships. *But by the same token, if you have worshipped often and regularly, then you will undoubtedly worship well in the hour of your greatest need.* [12]

The experience of worship provides the deep resources we need to draw upon when everything around falls apart. In worship, the emphasis and focus is not upon the person but upon God. Do you realize that your theology will affect how you respond to loss? Your response to life's losses will be directly determined by your understanding of God and how you have worshiped.

We are people who usually put faith in formulas. We feel comfortable with predictability, regularity, and assurance. We want God to be this way also, and so we try to create Him in the image of what we want Him to be and what we want Him to do.

However, you and I cannot predict what God will do. Paul

reminds us of that in Romans 11:33 KJV: "O the depth of the riches both of the wisdom and knowledge of God! how unsearchable are his judgments, and his ways past finding out!"

God is not noncaring or busy elsewhere. He is neither insensitive nor punitive. He is supreme, sovereign, loving, and sensitive.

I don't fully comprehend God. I too have unanswered questions about some of the events of my life. But all of life's trials, problems, crises, and suffering occur by divine permission. As Don Baker puts it:

> God allows us to suffer. This may be the only solution to the problem that we will ever receive. Nothing can touch the Christian without having first received the permission of God. If I do not accept that statement, then I really do not believe that God is sovereign—and if I do not believe in His sovereignty, then I am helpless before all the forces of heaven and hell.[13]

God allows suffering for His purpose and for His reasons. He gives permission. This should help us see God as the gracious Controller of the universe. God is free to do as He desires . . . and He doesn't have to give us explanations or share His reasons. He doesn't owe us. He has already given us His Son and His Holy Spirit to strengthen and guide us. We look at problems and losses and say "Why?" Jesus asks us to look at them and say, "Why not?"

What God allows us to experience is for our growth. God has arranged the seasons of nature to produce growth, and He arranges the experiences of the seasons of our lives for growth also. Some days bring sunshine and some bring storms. Both are necessary. He knows the amount of pressure we can handle. First Corinthians 10:13 tells us He will ". . . not let you be tempted beyond what you can bear" (NIV). But He does let us be tempted, feel pain, and experience suffering. He does not always give us what we think we need or want but what will produce growth.

A woman came to me for counseling some time ago. She had experienced a loss several months before and was upset because a friend had suggested she thank God for the problems she was experiencing.

"I can't believe she'd say that," the woman exclaimed. "That's ridiculous! It's insensitive! How can I thank God for this loss? It's disrupted my whole life!" She continued to vent her frustration.

After a while I said, "I wonder what she meant by her comment."

"What do you mean?" she replied.

"Well, did she mean to thank God for this specific loss as though it were good in and of itself, or to thank God for using this so that you have an opportunity to change and grow? Could that be it?"

"Well . . . I don't know," she ventured.

"I know it hurts, and you and your family wish it had never occurred," I said, "but it did. So the past can't be changed and you feel out of control. Perhaps you can't change what happens in the future, but you can control your response to whatever occurs. It's just something to think about."

She did think about it and in time she came to the place of thanking God for being with her and allowing her this time of growth.

"One day I thought about the choices I had," she said. "I could depend on God, thank Him, praise Him, and allow Him to work through me. This didn't seem so bad when I considered the alternative!"

What kind of growth can we expect? Lloyd Ogilvie suggests some of the things we can learn as we go through the difficult times in life that he calls valleys:

First, it has been in the valleys of waiting for answers to
my prayers that I have made the greatest strides in growing
in the Lord's grace.

Second, it's usually in retrospect, after the strenuous period is over, that I can look back with gratitude for what I've
received of the Lord Himself. I wouldn't trade the deeper
trust and confidence I experienced from the valley for a
smooth and trouble-free life.

Third, I long to be able to remember what the tough
times provide in my relationship with the Lord, so that
when new valleys occur, my first reaction will be to thank
and praise the Lord in advance for what is going to happen
in and through me as a result of what happens to me. I really
want my first thought to be, "Lord, I know You didn't send
this, but You have allowed it and will use it as a part of
working all things together for good. I trust You completely,
Lord!"[14]

This attitude doesn't negate the pain of a loss. When we have
suffered a loss, we feel like the disciples adrift in that small boat
during the storm on the Sea of Galilee. The waves throw us
about, and just as we get our legs under us, we're hit from
another direction. They struggled on the Sea of Galilee and we
struggle on the sea of life. All of us are afraid of capsizing. All
we see are waves that seem to grow larger each moment. We're
afraid. However, Jesus came to the disciples and He comes to us
today with the same message: "It is I; don't be afraid" (John
6:20 NIV).

We ask God, "Where are You?" but He is always there in the
midst of the crisis. We ask Him, "When? When will You answer?" As the Psalmist cried, "How long wilt thou forget me, O
Lord? for ever? How long wilt thou hide thy face from me? How
long shall I take counsel in my soul, having sorrow in my heart
daily? How long shall mine enemy be exalted over me?" (Psalms
13:1, 2 KJV). We want Him to act according to our timetable, but

the Scripture says, "Be still before the Lord and wait patiently for him" (Psalms 37:7 NIV). We become restless in waiting, and to block out the pain of waiting, we are often driven to frantic activity. This does not help, but resting before the Lord does:

> Often waiting is a time of darkening clouds. Our skies do not lighten. Instead, everything seems to become even more grim.
> Yet the darkening of our skies may forecast the dawn. It is in the gathering folds of deepening shadows that God's hidden work for us takes place. The present, no matter how painful, is of utmost importance.
> Somewhere, where our eyes cannot see and our ears are unable to hear, God is. And God is at work.[15]

You may not feel that God is doing anything to help you recover. Why? Because we want recovery *now*. The instant-solution philosophy of our society often invades a proper perspective of God. We complain about waiting a few weeks or days, but to God a day is as a thousand years and a thousand years an instant. God works in hidden ways, even when you and I are totally frustrated by His apparent lack of response. We are merely unaware that He is active. Hear the words of Isaiah for people then and now:

> Since ancient times no one has heard,
>   no ear has perceived,
> no eye has seen any God besides you,
>   who acts on behalf of those who wait for him.
> You come to the help of those who gladly do right,
>   who remember your ways.
>   Isaiah 64:4, 5 NIV

God has a reason for everything He does and a timetable for when He does it: " 'For I know the plans I have for you,' declares the Lord, 'plans to prosper you and not to harm you, plans to give you hope and a future' '' (Jeremiah 29:11 NIV). Give yourself permission not to know what, not to know how, and not to know when. Even though you feel adrift on the turbulent ocean, God is holding you and knows the direction of your drift. Giving yourself permission to wait can give you hope. It is all right for God to ask us to wait for weeks and months and even years. During that time when we do not receive the answer and/or solution we think we need, He gives us His presence: ''But I trust in you, O Lord; I say, 'You are my God.' My times are in your hands . . .'' (Psalms 31:14, 15 NIV).

The ability to develop a biblical perspective on our lives is perhaps best summarized in this verse: ''Consider it all joy, my brethren, when you encounter various trials, knowing that the testing of your faith produces endurance'' (James 1:2, 3 NAS).

It is easy to read a passage like this and say, ''Well, that's fine.'' It is another thing, however, to put it into practice.

What does the word *consider* actually mean? It refers to an internal attitude of the heart or mind that allows the trials and circumstances of life to affect us adversely or beneficially. Another way James 1:2 might be translated is, ''Make up your mind to regard adversity as something to welcome or be glad about.''

You have the power to decide what your attitude will be. You can approach it and say, ''That's terrible. Totally upsetting. That is the last thing I wanted for my life. Why did it have to happen now? Why me?''

The other way of considering the same difficulty is to say, ''It's not what I wanted or expected, but it's here. There are going to be some difficult times, but how can I make the best of them?'' Don't ever deny the pain or hurt you might have to go through, but always ask, ''What can I learn from it? How can I grow through this? How can it be used for God's glory?''

The verb tense used in the word *consider* indicates a decisiveness of action. It is not an attitude of resignation (''Well, I'll just give up. I'm stuck with this problem. That's the way life is."). If you resign yourself, you will sit back and not put forth any effort. The verb tense actually indicates you will have to go against your natural inclination to see the trial as a negative force. There will be some moments when you won't see it that way at all, and then you will have to remind yourself, "No, I think there is a better way of responding to this. Lord, I really want You to help me see it from a different perspective." Then your mind will shift to a more constructive response. Often, this takes a lot of work on your part.

God created us with both the capacity and the freedom to determine how we will respond to those unexpected incidents life brings our way. You may honestly wish a certain event had never occurred, but you cannot change the fact.

During times of crisis as well as all the other times of life, our stability comes from our Lord. God's Word says:

> Now to Him who is able to establish you according to my gospel and the preaching of Jesus Christ, according to the revelation of the mystery which has been kept secret for long ages past.
>
> Romans 16:25 NAS

> Then he said to them, "Go, eat of the fat, drink of the sweet, and send portions to him who has nothing prepared; for this day is holy to our Lord. Do not be grieved, for the joy of the Lord is your strength."
>
> Nehemiah 8:10 NAS

> And He shall be the stability of your times, A wealth of salvation, wisdom, and knowledge; The fear of the Lord is his treasure.
>
> Isaiah 33:6 NAS

Yes, recovery is possible. God wants us to recover, and He has provided a way for us to recover!

Notes

Chapter 8 Growing Through Our Losses

1. As quoted in Ann Kaiser Stearns, *Coming Back* (New York: Ballantine Books, 1988), 157.

2. Ibid., 172.

3. Ibid., 157–215, adapted.

4. Delores Kuenning, *Helping People Through Grief* (Minneapolis: Bethany House Publishers, 1987), 20, 21.

5. Dwight Carlson, *When Life Isn't Fair* (Eugene, Oregon: Harvest House Publishers, 1989), 38.

6. Ibid., 43.

7. Kuenning, *Helping People Through Grief*, 203. Quotation within this material is from Daniel Simundson, *Where Is God in My Suffering?* (Minneapolis: Augsburg Publishing House, 1983), 28, 29.

8. Carlson, *When Life Isn't Fair*, 52.

9. Harold Kushner, *When Bad Things Happen to Good People* (New York: Avon Books, 1981), 129.

10. C. S. Lewis, *The Problem of Pain* (London: Collins Publishers, 1961), 36.

11. John Killinger, *For God's Sake—Be Human* (Dallas, Texas: WORD Incorporated, 1970), 147. As quoted in Richard Exley, *The Rhythm of Life* (Tulsa: Honor Books, 1987), 108.

12. Exley, *Rhythm of Life*, 127, 137.

13. Don Baker, *Pain's Hidden Purpose* (Portland, Oregon: Multnomah Press, 1984), 72.

14. Lloyd John Ogilvie, *Why Not? Accept Christ's Healing and Wholeness* (Old Tappan, New Jersey: Fleming H. Revell Company, 1985), 162.

15. Larry Richards, *When It Hurts Too Much to Wait* (Dallas, Texas: WORD Incorporated, 1985), 67, 68.

9

The Loss of Identity: Who Am I?

She sat there looking quite desolate, her face reflecting the sense of loss that stormed within her. Soon she began to put into words what was so obvious from her expression:

> I thought I knew who I was. I've always seen myself as capable. I have a very prestigious career, which gives me a high status rating. I used to pride myself on that. But now it just doesn't seem enough. My job isn't fulfilling anymore. In the past, if someone asked me, "Who are you?" I could give a great answer, but it was always tied to my position in the company. I thought that was better than what I used to base my identity on. When I was younger, it was my looks. I was attractive and I knew it. I worked on it to get the most mileage out of it. One day I realized that eventually no matter what I did to look good, it wouldn't help. Age would catch up with me, and then what would I have? Who would I be? But now I'm floundering again. I don't really know who I am, and I feel empty and depressed over it.

Have you ever been there, in that bottomless pit, where you wondered who you were and no answers came? When it happens, it is frightening. We all need to have some meaning for who we are.

Any of us can suffer a loss of identity, but it is a loss that in most cases is preventable. That's right, it can be prevented. Many identity losses are felt because the source we base our identity upon is shaky.

Too often we think that striving for identity is an adolescent search. It should be over once we attain adulthood. But it isn't. Think about it for a minute. What do you base your identity upon? Don't you define yourself by your role or what you do? Don't you build who you are upon your emotional attachments to other people, places, and things? Do you base it upon your appearance? It is quite typical for people to do this, and that would be fine if life were static, certain, and always predictable. But it isn't.

Take a moment and write your response to the question, "Who are you?" Then come back to this chapter.

What did you write? Did you discover yourself expressing certain roles in your life? I often hear expressions such as, "I am a man," "I am a father," "I am a social worker," "I am a minister," "I am a widower," "I am a family person," "I am an athlete." But if you couldn't express who you are with these roles, what would you say?

At one of my seminars, I frustrate people because I ask them to introduce themselves to those around them and tell who they are, but they cannot mention what they do for a living. Just that simple instruction puts many of them into a state of conflict. If we do not have a broad basis for our identity, any kind of loss puts us into identity confusion. We have a mini identity crisis with each element that is taken away.

Who will you be when you are no longer a father?

Who will you be when you are no longer a social worker?

Who will you be when you are no longer a minister?

Who will you be when you are no longer a family person?

Who will you be when you are no longer an athlete?

Who will you be when you can no longer run or walk?

If we have no sense of who we are beyond our different roles in life, we have confined ourselves to a state of future identity confusion. However, it is possible for this loss to be avoided.

Who are the people you are attached to for your source of identity?

What are the things you are attached to for your identity?

How important are your house, your place of employment, your community standing, your car, and your clothing as sources for your identity?

What about your appearance? Does your identity fluctuate based upon how well you feel you look?

What about your performance? Does how you feel about yourself fluctuate based upon how well you did?

Whenever we build our identity on anything that is potentially changeable, what do you think that does to our identity? It makes us prone to experiencing not only the losses themselves but the potential loss of our identity as well.

Perhaps this startling fact will help us see how tenuous the foundations for our identity really are.

Suicide. An unpopular, highly avoided word. But it has a direct link to identity and loss. Nationally, 12 out of every 100,000 people take their lives.[1] But notice what happens with men as they age: the statistics change radically when men hit 65. For those in the age range of 65 to 74, 38 out of every 100,000 take their lives. And for those in the 75 to 84 age group, 57 out of every 100,000 take their lives. Why the sudden surge in the mid-sixties?

Loss of identity. Why? One major reason is the loss of employment. The word *retirement* generates mixed reactions. Work seems to have a multitude of meanings for people, especially men. Perhaps in the future we will see the same trend for women.

Research on the meaning of work has not turned up many new

findings over the past half century. The same observations made by Robert Havighurst in 1954 apply today. Naturally, work is there to provide a financial base for our lives. But here are some additional reasons for work. As you read them, consider these reasons in light of what meaning your occupation holds in your life.

Work is often used as the basis for our self-esteem or self-worth. Self-esteem increases when we feel good about what we accomplish on the job. It is part of the performance basis for identity. Work becomes more than a source of income, even though some people will cling to the belief that money is really the main motivating factor for a job. What happens if you are in a job that is based upon long-term projects with few visible indicators of how you are doing until the project is completed three years hence? What if you are in a sales job in which each week or month you start over, having to meet your quota and compete against all the other salespeople? This puts the self-esteem of some people on a roller coaster ride every week. There is little stability for their identity.

Where are you in this aspect of your life? Evaluate yourself on a scale of 0–10 as you consider the link between your self-esteem and your work.

0--------------------------------5--------------------------------10
Work is not the basis   Average   Work is the basis
for my self-esteem.   for my self-esteem.

Work is also a source for social life. Here is where we meet people, make lasting friendships, and have social interaction. Our job helps us network with others, and the socialization occurs even during working hours. But what happens when the job is no longer there? Do you take your friends with you? Do you have as much contact with them as when you worked together? Do they call you, or are you the one who has to stay in touch with them most of the time? If your identity is tied into these social relationships, how do you feel about yourself when this source dries up?

John had spent over two decades as a crossing guard. He was loved by scores of children and parents alike. In fact, the last two years he began to cross the young children of some of the former children from years before. Eventually, he found he could no longer carry out his duties.

"I miss those kids," he said. "I didn't have that much contact with many other folks, but twice a day I saw those kids, talked with them, and got to know their folks. Even when I wasn't on duty during Christmas vacation, I would receive cards and gifts from them. Those kids were my whole life. It gave me the friends and grandkids I never had. Now it's really lonely not getting to that corner each day."

What about you? To what extent do you base your identity upon your business social relationships and connections? Evaluate yourself using the same scale of 0–10.

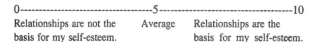

0---------------------------------5----------------------------------10
Relationships are not the   Average   Relationships are the
basis for my self-esteem.   basis for my self-esteem.

Work is also used as a source of status or prestige. The name of the firm, the size of our cubbyhole or office, how close the office is to the president, whether or not we have a secretary, our title, whether or not we are given a company car (and the kind of car!)—all of these factors are tied into status. Many people build their source of identity upon this foundation.

With a changing economy, war and the ever-present threat of new wars, inroads from foreign distributors and companies, and failing savings and loan companies, no profession or job is absolutely secure. All it could take is a small recession and the company car is recalled, the office vanishes, the sales territory is reshaped, and a new nebulous title is given that has little or no meaning. Then how do you feel about yourself? These losses can be devastating, especially if other people know about all that you have at work. The loss of face is an added blow. Evaluate to what extent work is your source of status and prestige.

```
0----------------------------------5----------------------------------10
```
Work is not my source   Average   Work is my source of
of status and prestige.   status and prestige.

Work has another meaning for most people. It is an opportunity to express yourself. You can achieve, be creative, and perhaps have some new experiences. For those who feel this way about their work, retirement is seen as an enemy rather than something to be anticipated. As one man said, "When I had to retire, I dried up inside. I stagnated. My avenue for expression was taken away."

Is work your source of expressing who you are? If so, what will happen when you retire? Perhaps now is the time to evaluate where you are.

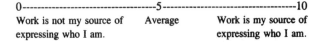

```
0----------------------------------5----------------------------------10
```
Work is not my source of   Average   Work is my source of
expressing who I am.   expressing who I am.

For a number of people, work is an opportunity to serve others. It is easy to think of a number of occupations that have serving as their basic purpose. But service can occur in most occupations because it is really based upon the attitude or motivation of the person. For some, serving others is a life's calling, and they seek out a profession that affords them that opportunity. But when they retire and their outlet is cut off, how do they handle this loss? For some, it is devastating. For others, it isn't a problem. Why? What is the difference? Perhaps it would help you to evaluate your own thoughts about your work. To what extent is it an expression of serving others?

```
0--------------------------------5------------------------------------10
Work is not my basis for      Average          Work is my basis for
serving others.                                serving others.
```

Finally, for a large number of people, work is simply an opportunity to fill time. It is their way of taking care of the mundane, humdrum part of life. Take away the job and they become bored. Some occupations do tend to lend themselves to this work attitude. But even if this is all work means, what happens when that mandatory age is reached or illness necessitates retirement? It too is a loss. Is your work a time filler? Evaluate yourself on this last purpose and then reflect on all six. What do your answers tell you about your identity and its source?

```
0--------------------------------5------------------------------------10
Work is not the basis for     Average          Work is the basis
filling my time.                               for filling my time.
```

The loss of identity based upon work does not happen only when the employment ceases. It can happen with the loss of the dream we originally had about our vocation. The young, aspiring actress who sees acting as giving her identity and meaning in life may discover the shallowness, manipulation, and conniving on the road to success in her profession, and her dream may be destroyed. The peace corps worker who dreamed of changing the future of a small tribe comes to realize that he or she will not be the one to make that happen.

The empty nest stage of the family life cycle, which we mentioned in Chapter 8, is an interesting adjustment. For some couples, the empty nest is a major loss. It can actually be a mingling of numerous feelings as expressed in Ecclesiastes 3:1–8: a time of weeping, laughing, mourning, healing, loving, releasing, losing, and relief. The atmosphere of the home changes. There are fewer choices to make, less confusion and noise. Patterns of shopping, cooking, and scheduling will change. I have several relatives who have raised large families on farms. The mothers were used to cooking large meals for their brood. But the day comes when that role is no longer needed. New roles must be established, and often new pressures are felt. Needs formerly filled by children will be diverted to others for fulfillment. Sometimes an additional loss occurs if the couple lunges toward each other to fill the empty spaces in their lives. They may end up pushing each other away because of their intensity, and a feeling of abandonment can result.

If a couple has relied upon the children to hold their relationship together or to give them something to focus on, the leaving of the last child creates an enormous loss within the marital relationship as well. The mother who has relied upon her role as the primary source of her self-identity may end up feeling abandoned, unloved, uncared for, and depressed. If she gave up a career to have children, the loss of the last child can elicit resentment.

If a woman's role is that of a mother, the leaving of the last child is accompanied by the removal of her identity. Thus this transition brings the loss of the dependent child and the loss of identity. It could also bring to light the fact that intimacy has been absent in the marriage for many years, for the camouflage is no longer there. A working mother often has an easier time adjusting because she already has another outlet that helps her cope with her loss.

The empty nest also affects fathers. A child who was Mother's little girl at six may have become Dad's special pal. When she leaves, he could feel devastated. The leaving of a child also points out to him that life could be passing him by too fast.

The man who for years has sold his identity to the pursuit of a dream through his vocation finally hits a brick wall. Sometime in mid-life, he realizes that he is never really going to attain his goal and fulfill his dream. Or maybe he has arrived at his goal and says, "So what? There's got to be more than this. Is this all?" A sense of loss and emptiness sets in. The man who has lived a solitary life without close male friends, has never learned to experience or express his feelings, and has built his identity upon his work is the one who is most prone to experience the classic, male mid-life crisis.

All men go through mid-life transition that has the potential for growth, new direction, and new life. It is all right to evaluate, question, and ultimately discover a new sense of purpose.

There are many women today who build their identity through performance, appearance, or being a mother. They too come to the place where the feeling, "Is this all there is?" may hit. Or they are confronted with diminishing performance and appearance, or the children leave home. Unfortunately, more attention has been given to men's mid-life transitions than to transitions for women, which may mean less help or understanding is available.

Dreams. The substance of life is made up of dreams and desires. We need them. Our society needs them. It is out of dreams that people are motivated, new inventions and approaches come about, and people feel a purpose. That is why when a dream dies it can be so devastating.

We seem to feel that most dreams come from those who are young. Remember what your dreams were when you were young? Perhaps they had to do with your vocation, or with the amount of money you were going to make. Maybe your dream was about something you would create.

For example, I always wanted to live where I could experience a forest and the seasons. Finally, at the age of fifty, a portion of that dream has come true, but not in the way that I dreamed.

I had friends in high school who dreamed of what they were going to achieve. As I reflect on some of my dreams and theirs, I realize there were two categories of dreams: realistic and unrealistic. What about your dreams? Which ones have come true? Which did you give up? What are your dreams at the present time? It seems that as our youth diminishes, so do our dreams. Some of them won't ever come true. People in mid-life have to face the fact that some of their vocational dreams will never come true.

In my counseling office, I often hear about dreams. Some of them are attainable. Others are mere fantasies that will never make it in the real world. So often, I hear about a wife's dream of having a happy and fulfilled marriage, and how that dream crumbled when her partner walked out the door.

The older we become, the less we dream, since we have less energy, time, and even desire. Letting go of some of these dreams is part of becoming realistic adults. Judith Viorst talks about the "necessary losses" in her book of that title. We need to experience some losses in order to move into the next phase of life. She describes the loss of dreams that accompanies our journey through middle age:

> And we may start to feel that this is a time of always letting go, of one thing after another after another: Our waistlines. Our vigor. Our sense of adventure. Our 20/20 vision. Our trust in justice. Our earnestness. Our playfulness. Our dream of being a tennis star, or a TV star or a senator or the woman for whom Paul Newman finally leaves Joanne. We give up hoping to read all the books we once had vowed to read, and to visit all the places we'd once vowed to visit. We give up hoping we'll save the world from

cancer or from war. We even give up hoping that we will succeed in becoming underweight—or immortal.[2]

Jim Conway points out a similar issue as men face mid-life:

How he evaluates his past accomplishments, hopes and dreams will determine whether his life ahead will be an exhilarating challenge for him or simply a demoralizing distance that must be drearily traversed. In either case, he is at a time of trauma, because his emotions, as never before, are highly involved.[3]

Is it easy to give up a dream? Not really. Dreams give us hope and inspiration. They may not be as visual as having a car totaled in an accident, but they are real.

Have you ever thought about how your identity is tied into your dreams? Take away your dreams, and who are you? How do lost dreams affect how you feel about yourself? Giving up a dream calls you to the reality that not only do you not have the ability or time to achieve this dream but also that someday you won't even be here! There is an ending to this earthly life.

Not all of our dreams have to be profound. I grew up with music. I played piano, clarinet, bass clarinet, and saxophone. I had many enjoyable experiences in bands and orchestras. But I always wanted to play the trumpet. It was a dream and a desire of mine, especially when I heard some of the greats.

One day when I was about forty-eight, I was thinking about my wish to play the trumpet. Then I thought, *Well, what's keeping you from playing?* And I responded, *Nothing.* So I found a teacher, rented a trumpet (and eventually purchased one), and for a few years I took lessons. Then I stopped, for several reasons. I had learned enough to play some tunes (in key), and that was fulfilling. In fact, it was a real boost to me when the dogs quit leaving the room when I practiced. But in addition to being fulfilled, the realities of what I wanted to do hit me as well. At my age, my lip muscles were not going to respond as well as if I had started when I was a child. I didn't have the amount of time to put in each day to achieve the level I had once dreamed of when I was younger. Putting all of that together helped me make my decision to stop. I had realized a dream, although not to the extent of what it was at one time. This is a process that all of us have to face in many areas of our lives as we become older.

Growing older doesn't have to mean the death of our dreams. They can be revised, reshaped, and refashioned to meet the reality of who and what we are as well as our abilities. I have met people in their fifties, sixties, and seventies who still had dreams. These people are survivors.[4]

The loss of dreams troubles us because it is an indication that we are moving from one of the idols of our society—"being youthful"—to a level of toleration—"being old." Even with the graying of America, it is still a tolerated state. R. Scott Sullender summarizes it so well:

> In American society "old" carries a negative connotation and "young" has a positive flavor. Old is considered obsolete, useless, out of date. Old appliances are thrown out, old clothes are discarded. Old technology is not cost efficient and so it is replaced. This is a disposal society. When it gets old, throw it away. Little wonder then that older people feel as though they are being thrown away too. Their advice is not sought after. They are isolated from the mainstream of society. They are now useless, the "discards" of society.[5]

Not only must we grieve over the loss of some of our dreams but additionally, many people have never faced the reality of the loss of their youth and have failed to grieve for that. Who is it that dictates to us what we should believe about youth? There are positives and negatives to every phase of life. Denying aging is denying the life process that God created. Perhaps we don't always like what happens. Perhaps we would have done it differently if we had been in charge of the creation of the human race. But the more we fight it, the more we feel out of control.

As with a number of losses that occur in life, the transition from being young to middle-aged to old is a gradual journey. There will be days when it isn't even evident to you, and then there will be days when you cry out, "I must be getting older." Your body tells you so. Every time you experience that discovery of the aging process you will need to face it and deal with it. Seeing our lives through God's eyes can help us make better sense of what is happening to us. Grieving for each stage and each loss keeps us fully alive. Think about this:

> We should not "borrow from the future" by living in fear of the next life stage. Neither should we live in the past by "idolizing" the life stage just completed. Live fully in the present. Enjoy it. Embrace it. Look for God there. However, in order to fully embrace the present, we must regularly let go of the past, and one of the most significant losses that we must periodically let go of is the loss of our youth.[6]

Think with me about your future, no matter what your age. When you retire, what are the voids you will experience in your life? Consider the list again:

loss of self-esteem
loss of social life
loss of status or prestige
loss of creativity or expression
loss of opportunity to serve others
loss of time fulfillment

Which of these will you grieve over?

Everyone varies in the losses they experience at retirement. I have seen some who lose all six, some the first two or three, some the last three, and some none! Why the variation? Does this mean that these losses are preventable? Yes!

The meaning that you attach to your work will make the difference. I have seen people in my office who no longer work because they were fired, disabled, experienced bankruptcy, or retired. Regardless of the reason for their loss of work, some were devastated and some weren't. It all went back to the meaning they attached to their work.

We are people who tend toward idolatry. We create idols and build our lives around them. For many, the body and how it looks is an idol. For some, it is wealth and possessions. For numerous mothers, the calling to be a mother becomes an idol. And for many, whether they realize it or not, their work is an idol. When something becomes everything to us, that is idolatry.

Let's consider work again. Our work is meant to be an expression of who we are as God's handiwork. Because of who God is and how He sees us, as evidenced in the gift of His Son, Jesus Christ, we must be worth something. We have value, worth, dignity, and adequacy because God has declared that we have them. Instead of our work giving us a sense of value, worth, dignity, and adequacy as Christians, it is the other way around.

The *way* we do our job is an expression of the high value God has ascribed to us.

The *proficiency* of the level of our work is an expression of the high value God has ascribed to us.

We bring *dignity* to our work because of God's giving us a sense of dignity. As believers, we have the opportunity to do a job out of the sense of *adequacy* we have because of God's declaration that we are adequate. We should not be using our work to make us feel adequate. If we search the Scriptures, we discover that we are special and worthwhile only because of God.

Over the centuries, we have used many means in our attempts

to feel worthwhile, but they are all temporary. None are permanent, except for God's declaration. This is the initial step in preventing or lessening our sense of loss when our work is no longer available to us. It is the same step in preventing or lessening our sense of loss when our ability, looks, or position in life is no longer a part of our life.

What would happen to you and the quality of your work if your attitude was this: My work is an expression of me and the presence of God in my life! It would be the beginning of feeling good about yourself in spite of what is going on at your job.

If our friendships are basically formed at work and not outside of work, we have been taken captive by the limitations of the job. Selecting friends from many sources gives us the opportunity to be in charge of this selection instead of having it just occur. This can help to prevent a possible future loss.

Those who broaden the base for their prestige are able to handle the diminished source when the job is gone. We all need some basis for prestige. The risk comes when it is based upon some element that is transitory.

Creativity can be used in many areas of life. Look around you. Consider all the opportunities that are either already there or that you can discover to express your abilities. Look around your church and neighborhood, talk to others, search through your library. You may be surprised at what you discover.

Serving others does not have to be limited to work. There are probably more opportunities for service outside of work than within it. Not working does not have to curtail this potential in any way.

I have difficulty with work used as an excuse to pass time and give a person something to do. There is so much to do all around us. I have talked to many people who couldn't wait for retirement so they could get on with their lives. They were going to be even busier than when they were employed full-time.

Usefulness, meaning in life, and creativity are not limited to work. Loss of a job for any reason does constitute a loss, but you can think of it more as a transition. Be in charge of the extent of this loss. Viewing it as a transition *from* one opportunity *to* another gives purpose and direction.[7]

You see, the question is not, "Who are you in light of your work?" It's who are you spiritually. The real question is, "Who are you, really?" The answer is "His!" You belong not to yourself. You belong to Him.

Retirement is just one of the precipitating causes for an identity loss. The older we become, the more we are at risk for a loss. A major identity loss facing many older people is one that occurs when the home that has been lived in for many years is sold.

My mother moved to California in 1918 and built her first home in the hills above Hollywood. She subsequently built three other homes and lived there until 1978. But she still retained one of her houses, the one I grew up in. Because she was one of the pioneers who settled in Laurel Canyon, and because she built two homes with her own hands and kept those homes in repair for almost sixty years, her identity was wrapped up in her property and homes. When she finally came to the time in her life to sell, it was the final step in an identity transition. She was no longer a resident or a home owner in Laurel Canyon. Her identity is now tied in to a retirement community.

When you live in a home for over half a century, the move is much more than shifting from one house to another. Many roles have been lived out there. The major issues and changes of life have been experienced there. A person's history is tied into a home. When people move, voluntarily or otherwise, roots are pulled out of the ground.

One of the statements we hear from those who are older is, "They didn't do it that way when I was that age." The changing of generations is an identity loss. I never thought I would arrive at that place, but already I am noticing values I feel are important disappearing with the new generation. I notice that levels of commitment are not what they used to be. The desire for immediate gratification that is taught throughout the media is seen in people wanting to start out with what it took the previous generation twenty-five years of hard work to attain.

We notice the loss of our generation in two ways: the changes that occur within society itself and the loss of our peers and friends around us. As we move past fifty, deaths of contemporaries and relatives become much more frequent. The passing on of friends and relatives is a very crucial stage for us, but have you ever thought of it as a major stage of loss in your life? As people die or even move away, we feel a sense of loneliness and isolation. We are faced with the fact of our mortality. We need other people, and often we fail to replace those who have left us. If we have friends who are cross-generational, we do not feel the loss as much.

Who are your friends? What happens when they leave your life? Even the breakup of a friendship can be a devastating loss. I have five close male friends. I relate in a different way to each one of them. From a professional interaction level to a fishing companion to a racquetball partner, the ties we have to one another are varied. Some I see each week and the others infrequently, except for phone contacts. The loss of any one of them would leave a void in my life.

When you lose a friend, you lose more than the person. You lose your routine and certain roles as well.[8]

What is the basis for your identity? Is it a foundation that is not subject to erosion as time goes on? The normal losses we all experience will be handled so much better when our identity is in Christ and we see ourselves from God's perspective—valued, loved, and sufficient because of Him. We hear much today about the difficulties of being a dependent person. The reality is that we have been called to be dependent people—not upon others or ourselves but upon God. When we are, we become not just survivors or maintainers but conquerors as well. This is the truth of Scripture. It is the truth of what life is all about.

Notes

Chapter 9 The Loss of Identity: Who Am I?

1. Gloria Jaufman Koenig, "Helping No. 1 Suicide Risk . . . Elderly Men," *Los Angeles Times,* November 15, 1984, and "Suicide— Retired Professor Chooses Death," March 16, 1989, adapted.

2. Judith Viorst, *Necessary Losses* (New York: Simon & Schuster, Inc., 1986), 269.

3. Jim Conway, *Men in Mid-Life Crisis* (Elgin, Illinois: David C. Cook Publishing Co., 1978), 17, 18.

4. R. Scott Sullender, *Losses in Later Life* (New York: Paulist Press, 1989), 43–47, adapted.

5. Ibid., 45, 46.

6. Ibid., 51.

7. Ibid., 94–107.

8. Ibid., 157, adapted.

10
The Loss of a Relationship

Heartbreak, disappointment, loneliness, numbness—these are words that describe our feelings when we experience broken friendships, broken engagements, and broken marriages. In addition, every survivor of a broken relationship is haunted by a residue of fear about future relationships. Some people face breakups squarely, learn from them, override their fears, and grow to trust and love again. But others allow their emotional wounds to remain perpetually open; they give in to their fears by withdrawing from intimate relationships. The trauma of love lost is one of life's most painful hurts, and the apprehension about loving again is one of life's greatest fears.

When you have trusted another person with your feelings of love and affection, and the relationship ends, your life seems to come to a standstill for a while. Usually the first love lost is the most painful. Some of the men and women who hurt the most are those who are still deeply attached to former spouses or fiancés and want the relationships to be restored. They feel desperate, totally out of control, and willing to do almost anything to keep their partners. But they have no control over the decisions of loved ones.

Being out of control in any situation is fearful, but having no control over a broken relationship is intensely fearful. Watching your loved one slip away without any recourse leaves you feeling empty and impotent. You feel as if you are unraveling emotionally.

When the loss of a spouse occurs, fear of the future begins to come in waves. Lynn Caine described the beginning of her grief:

> When the protective fog of numbness had finally dissipated, life became truly terrifying. I was full of grief, choked with unshed tears, overwhelmed by the responsibility of bringing up two children alone, panicked about my financial situation, almost immobilized by the stomach-wrenching, head-splitting pain of realizing that I was alone. My psychic pain was such that putting a load of dirty clothes in the washing machine, taking out the vacuum cleaner, making up a grocery list, all the utterly routine household chores, loomed like Herculean labors.[1]

Once your intimate relationship ends, a part of you wants to try again with a new relationship. But another part of you says, "Don't! It isn't worth the risk!" You are afraid the past will recur and your new relationship will also end in a painful breakup. Or you are afraid you will always feel the loss and pain of your previous breakup and never be able to reach out and love again. This fear is intensified whenever you relive the breakup. Every time the painful scenario replays in your memory, the emotional sledgehammer crashes down on you again. For some, this fear can bring on panic attacks. I have even heard people say they thought they were going crazy during this phase.

The fear of reliving the past paralyzes the normal process of building a new relationship. This fear creates a hesitancy to invest energy, love, and transparency in a new love interest. Many people who are afraid to move ahead in a new relationship are also afraid to remain behind without anyone to love. They feel trapped between the fear of loving again and the fear of never being loved again.

Even the loss created by a broken friendship can be devastating. I have experienced that twice in my adult life, and it was painful to wonder what went wrong. It is fortunate when you have several close friends to help you through the loss. But for the person who has only one or two close friends, the severance of a relationship can feel like a death.

There are additional emotions that feed the fear of loving again. One of them is guilt—the feeling that you have failed yourself, your ideals, your Lord, or the other person. This guilt may exist whether you were the *rejected* person or the *rejecting* person. Unresolved guilt damages self-esteem, and low self-esteem produces greater fear. If you feel guilty about a broken relationship, it is important to identify whether the feelings are based on reality (such as breaking a commitment or acting irresponsibly toward the other person) or imagination (taking the blame for something that was not really your responsibility).

Why do these broken relationships hit us so hard? Part of the happiness that comes from a close, loving relationship is being loved by the other person. Consider the parent-child relationship. Usually it is a two-way love relationship. If your father (or mother) dies, you know he didn't die because he stopped caring for you. He simply died, and you accept that. When a pet dies or even runs away, you realize that it wasn't because your pet didn't care for you.

But when a relationship breaks up, it is different. The love and care that once existed for you has dried up. It has vanished into thin air. The person still exists. You still may see each other regularly or occasionally at work. That makes it even more difficult. And what if he or she begins to date your best friend? Or marries your friend?

I've heard of many painful aftermaths of breakups. One girl's fiancé broke up with her and married her sister. How do you imagine she felt? Another young woman was dating a fifty-year-old man who was crazy about her. One day he introduced her to his twenty-eight-year-old son. Five weeks later, she and the son were married.

When breakups occur, you long for the relationship you once had. For some, this longing becomes an obsession dominating every waking moment. Nothing has any meaning until that relationship is restored, but restoration of the relationship exactly as it was happens very infrequently. The feeling of being out of control is particularly devastating, since there is nothing you can do. You can beg, plead, offer bribes, threaten suicide, and so on, all to no avail. Nothing seems to work, nothing will work, and nothing does work. You feel abandoned, forsaken, betrayed, and all alone.

Like the grief we experience when a person dies, the stages you will go through to recover from a lost relationship are predictable. These stages constitute the normal and healthy process of recovery. If the healing is complete, you will have some emotional scars but no open emotional wounds. I have talked to some people who still had oozing wounds from a relationship for over fifteen years. That's sad.

Please keep in mind that the stages identified here vary in their length and intensity, depending upon the duration and strength of the relationship. When the breakup is not your doing or desire, the result is even more intense.

There are usually six stages you will go through when a love relationship falls apart. Your pain will be the greatest during the first three stages. As you move through each stage, the intensity of your pain will diminish. The further along the path you proceed, the less fear you will experience. The worst thing to have happen is to get stuck in a stage and not complete the process.

Some of these stages overlap, and you may move back and

forth between them for a while. This is quite normal. It is a part of the healing process.

Stage One: Shock. When you first lose a love relationship, you feel dumfounded and overwhelmed by shock. Even when the breakup or divorce has been anticipated, the reality of it has a unique effect. Some people are unable to carry on their day-to-day activities; even eating and sleeping are chores. You live by your feelings at this stage.

Whether or not you can identify it, you will experience an intense fear of being alone or of being abandoned forever. But you need to experience these feelings in order to move through the healing process. At this stage, you need to have other people around you, whether or not you feel like having them around. Just the presence of other people can help ease the fear of loneliness.

Stage Two: Grief. The grief stage may be extensive since it includes mourning the loss of what you shared together and what you *could have* shared together. During this time, the anger mentioned earlier may be felt and expressed. You may be angry at yourself, at God, and at others who don't understand your grief. You may become depressed about the broken relationship and the hopelessness of relationships in the future.

When the ended relationship is a divorce, this is the time when certain "divorce myths" rear their heads. The first is "Nobody understands." It is the feeling that your situation is so unique and unusual, it is inconceivable to think anyone else could understand. It is important to realize that those who have gone through this do understand every aspect of it. They understand the feelings of abandonment, self-blame, other-blame, anger, guilt, the knifelike anguish and pain.

"I am going to die" is a predominant feeling. Everything is seen through this filter. But as one person described it, "Do I hurt a great deal at this time? Yes. Do I wish I were dead? Yes. Do I wish I could die? No."[2]

Many people experience mild paranoia. Statements like, "Everyone is talking about me," "I'm the subject of their conversations," "I can tell they're avoiding me," and "No one wants to be around me," are frequently made. Unfortunately, the person often believes these statements, and worse yet, in some narrow, unloving churches, they are sometimes true. Emotional sensitivity is heightened at this time, and becoming self-conscious is common.

Other common ideas of divorced people are, "Everybody hates me," "God hates me," and "He is so displeased with me." These thoughts are just not true. God hates the act of divorce, but He does not hate the divorced person. When others respond to you differently, it is not because of a defect in you. They could be self-conscious because they don't know what to say. After all, who has ever given us guidelines on how to respond when someone goes through a broken relationship![3]

In addition to these thoughts, an entire range of symptoms may begin to reside in you. Obsessional thinking begins to take you prisoner. It is a sign of hanging on to the relationship.

Do any of the following relate to your past or present life?

You arrange "accidental meetings" with the other person.

Your thought life is consumed by the other person.

You listen for the telephone and run for it when it rings.

You listen to sad songs and think they are about you and the one you lost.

You think you see your former love or his or her car everywhere.

You want to contact the person but you are afraid of rejection.

You follow people or cars thinking it is the person you lost.

You spend a great amount of time thinking about the person, devising plans of what to say or how to get him or her back, or wondering if what he said when you were together was untrue.

You just know that this relationship was the best one you could ever have.

What other thoughts do you have? Perhaps it would help to make a list of them and take steps to put them to rest.[4]

Thought stopping is a necessary step so that reality has a chance to gain a foothold in your life once again. Notice the negative thoughts of this woman who was rejected and how she countered each one to bring her life back into balance. You may find it beneficial to monitor and chart your own thoughts.

Negative thoughts	*Answers*
He shouldn't have left me for another woman.	I don't like it, but he should have left because he did. For all the reasons I don't know of, he should have left. I don't have to like it, just accept it.
I need him.	I want him back, but I don't need him. I need food, water, and shelter to survive. I don't need a man to survive. Thinking in terms of "needs" makes me vulnerable.
This always happens to me, and it will never change.	Just because it happened in one case doesn't mean it has happened or will happen in every case.
This is terrible, awful, horrible.	These are labels I add to the facts. The labels don't change anything, and they make me feel worse.
I must have someone to love me.	It's nice to love and be loved, but making it a condition to happiness is a way of putting myself down.
I'm too ugly and too fat to find anyone else.	"Too" is a relative concept, not some absolute standard. Thinking like this is self-defeating and stops me from trying.

I can't stand being alone.	I can stand difficulties—as I have in the past. I just don't like them.
I made a fool out of myself.	There's no such thing as a fool. Foolishness is only an abstraction, not something that exists. This mislabeling doesn't do me any good and makes me feel bad.
He made me depressed.	No one can make me feel depressed. I make myself depressed by the way I'm thinking.[5]

When you have thoughts that continue to return again and again, there is hope. They *can* be evicted from your life. There are two specific steps to take. First, pray out loud, sharing your concern, and describe specifically what you want God to do with these thoughts. Second, read aloud the following passages, which talk about how we can control our thought life: Isaiah 26:3; Ephesians 4:23; Colossians 3:1, 2; 2 Corinthians 10:5; Philippians 4:6–9.

Identify one of the most persistent or upsetting thoughts, the one that pops into your head more frequently than any of the others. Now select a time when you are not upset. Say the statement or statements out loud without crying or becoming angry. If you can't, that's all right. In time, you will be able to do this. When you say the last word of the statement (such as, "How could she have been so deceptive and *unfair?*"), slam a book or ruler loudly on a table or just clap your hands. Repeat the sentence and move the noise back one word each time you repeat the bothersome thought. In time, this thought will be interrupted before it has a chance to begin. And as this happens, thank God for taking this thought from your life.[6]

Stage Three: Blame. Feelings of blame, accompanied by anger, may be held toward your former spouse, fiancée, or dating partner—or even toward yourself. Your behavior during this

stage may surprise you as you attempt to rid yourself of these
feelings. Your actions may not seem to fit your past patterns. You
may engage in compulsive behaviors such as shopping or eating
binges, alcohol abuse, or even promiscuity. It is not unusual for
people to make poor decisions at this stage. Fears of rejection,
isolation, or personal inadequacy prompt some people to act contrary to their own value systems.

Jim was a thirty-five-year-old whose wife divorced him to
marry her employer. Jim was devastated by the divorce, but
gradually he began to date again. However, he was quite unsuc-
cessful in his new relationships.

One day Jim explained:

> I guess I'm still angry at my wife for leaving me. But
> there's no way I can make her pay for what she did to me,
> and I can't take my anger out on her. So that's probably
> why these new relationships aren't working out. I like the
> women I date, but I don't treat them well. I get angry at
> them, and I'm often rude. That's just not me! I guess I'm
> trying to get back at my wife by taking my anger out on
> these other women. And that isn't good for them or for me.
> I guess I try to hurt them first because I'm afraid they may
> hurt me the way my wife did. And I don't ever want to be
> hurt like that again!

Fortunately, Jim had the insight to figure out what he was
doing, and eventually he moved out of this stage.

During the grief and blame stages, some common mistakes can
hinder recovery. Generalizing after any broken relationship is so
easy to do. You take one isolated belief or experience and make
it apply to life in general. How many times I've heard my counselees say, "All women are money-minded," "All men are losers," "All men are sex animals," "All women are full of
emotions. They can't think." Such generalizations become im-
mobilizers.

A frequent mistake is falling into the trap of living by a self-fulfilling prophecy. Perhaps you have heard it or said it: "I'll never find anyone else. I'm stuck in life. I'll always be single now." This faulty belief blinds us from seeing the possibilities around us. It gives us an attitude and look of defeat. Our self-fulfilling prophecy says more about where we are coming from than where we are going.

These prophecies do nothing but undermine and cripple relationships.

Another mistake we tend to carry over from a broken relationship is a set of unrealistic expectations. We use words like *should* and *must*, and when things don't happen according to our rigid set of beliefs, we perpetuate a life of disappointment. We use expectations for ourselves and for other people:

"I have to be perfect for anyone to love me."

"If I don't meet all his needs, he won't love me."

"If she cares about me, she will . . . and she won't. . . ."

"If he reminds me of my former spouse or dating partner, he's not worth being with."

Wallowing in self-pity is an emotional trap that frequently follows a severed relationship. But indulging in self-pity blocks recovery and keeps others from getting close.

One of the most destructive responses is not being able to look in the mirror. One day a man in my office made the statement, "Norm, I can't bear to face myself after what's happened in my life." Sometimes these people are best referred to as runners. They are continually on the go and doing things to avoid having to deal with their situation and their feelings. They don't want to face themselves. The familiar patterns are incessant working, playing, being out each night, sleeping, watching T.V., and worse yet, moving into alcohol and drugs. The frantic, hectic, busy life is just as bad as a withdrawn, lethargic existence.[7]

A very common mistake designed both to overcome the pain of the loss and to strike back is "revenge loving." The hurt person plunges into a new relationship prematurely out of anger. This revenge could manifest itself in three different styles.

One manifestation is to engage in a new relationship simply to make the other person jealous. A tremendous amount of energy is expended in this approach because arrangements are made so the ex-fiancée or spouse actually sees the new couple.

Another variation of revenge loving is acting out toward the new person in your life the way you were treated by your former partner. If abuse was part of the history and you were the victim, the tables are now turned. If manipulation was the pattern, in order not to be hurt again this becomes your weapon and defense.

A final variation of revenge loving is developing a relationship in which you are in control so no one can ever control and hurt you again. But in all three of these revenge styles, both you and the new person end up hurt, unhappy, and dissatisfied.

There is a better way of draining anger. Revenge just doesn't work. In one of his articles on forgiveness, Lewis Smedes said that revenge is never paid back because alienated people keep track of their wrongs with different scorecards. Resentment punishes us more than the other person since most often the other individual isn't aware of the intensity of our feelings. Later we'll talk about how to get rid of anger in a constructive way.

Remember when you looked through a magnifying glass at a spider or some ferocious bug? It looked so large and threatening! Magnification is one of the traps and mistakes that occurs after a broken relationship. You begin to think about the man you lost and are convinced he is having the time of his life while you are living in despair and discouragement. You feel limited and constrained, while you are sure your ex is living life to the fullest. The major phrase in your vocabulary is, ''He is probably . . .'' or ''She is probably. . . .''

Magnification can easily lead to martyrdom—if you let it. We all have a choice in how we respond.

Rebounding is a term basketball fans are familiar with. But the kind of rebounding often found in broken relationships is best illustrated by throwing a racquetball against the wall of a small room in your home. It bounces erratically back and forth from wall to wall. Many people move into rebounding after a relationship. One young woman described the process in my counseling office:

> I feel as though I'm on a combination merry-go-round, bumper cars, and roller coaster all rolled up into one. I have to be on the go constantly or I think I'll go bananas. I'm always doing something and jumping into one relationship after another—and unfortunately, one bed after another. I don't like myself for doing this and it makes me feel even worse about the relationship I lost. I've decided to find some more constructive things to do with my time and to stay home on Thursday and Friday night each week to prove that I'm able to do it. It hurts, but I think I'll recover by doing this and I'm sure I can grow through this experience. I don't want to be chained to him forever, and I think I have been.

Another problem I have seen is idealization. I have heard both rejecters and rejectees make the same statement. For the rejecters, it was a rationalization of why they broke off the relationship with the other person. For the rejectees, it was a means of deadening the pain of the loss. The statement? "That person really had a lot of problems and defects. She [he] wasn't who or what she [he] said. In the long run, I think it's better that I look around and find someone else."

But the image they have of this new person is totally unrealistic. I have had some people make a list of the qualities they want. On one occasion I looked at the list and said, "Please let me know when you find this person. I didn't know someone like this even existed." Often I've wondered if this excessive standard wasn't set to protect them from ever having another relationship. They would never find such a person.

On the other hand, I have seen many people choose men or women just like their former partners, defects and all. These replacements will probably be just as disappointing as the previous partners were. But something drives them to prove that they can have relationships with people like this. Perhaps it is to prove to themselves and their former partners that the defect wasn't in them. This is why many daughters who have nonaffirming, aloof, distant fathers choose husbands who are very much like their fathers.[8]

Stage Four: Good-bye. This stage is often difficult to face, for it involves saying good-bye. This is when you really finally admit to yourself, "The relationship is over; this person is out of my life, and I have to go on." I have seen numerous people get stuck on the threshold of this stage, sometimes for more than a year. Some of them seem to move ahead, yet three weeks later they are asking the same questions and making the same statements about a reconciliation that will never happen. They are unwilling to say the final good-bye.

How do you say good-bye? Some of the same suggestions given in the chapter on saying good-bye when a loved one dies can be applied here.

Here are additional suggestions that are applicable to a broken relationship.

Let's consider anger and resentment. Perhaps the initial step in overcoming anger and resentment is to take inventory and identify the hurt, anger, and resentment. One divorced man wrote:

> I am so angry at you for your lies and infidelities.
> I resent the fact that I have to pay you spousal support. It should be the other way around for what you did.
> I am wounded by your betrayal of me and our wedding vows.

I am angry that you have the kids and they are being
influenced by your lousy life-style and lack of morals.

Often, when a person begins listing these resentments, buried
hurts and feelings begin climbing through the barriers. This list is
for your own use and is not to be shared with anyone else except
God. This is not an easy experience. You may find it very emotionally draining.

After you have made your list, go into a room and set up two
chairs facing each other. Sit in one chair and imagine the other
person is sitting opposite you listening to what you are sharing.
Read your list out loud with your tone and inflections registering
the feelings you have. Don't be concerned about editing what you
are saying. Just get it out. Some people keep their list for days,
adding to it as things come to mind. Others find it helpful to sit
down and share like this several times for the drainage benefits.
Don't be surprised to find yourself feeling angry, depressed,
intense, embarrassed, or anxious. When you have concluded your
time of sharing, spend a few minutes in prayer sharing these
feelings with God and thanking Him for understanding what you
are experiencing and for His presence in your life to help you
overcome the feelings.

To become a free person and move forward in life, there is one
additional step involved in the relinquishment of your anger and
resentment. It is called forgiveness. No one can tell you when it
will happen. You cannot hurry it up, for it too is a process that
takes time.

Most of us have our own set of reasons for not forgiving
another person. We object to letting him or her off the hook, as
it were. One of the ways to allow forgiveness to have a place in
your life is to identify the objections you have to forgiving the
person who hurt you so much.

Take a blank sheet of paper and write a salutation at the top.
Use the name of your former partner: "Dear_____". Underneath

the salutation, write the words, "I forgive you for_____". Then complete the sentence by stating something your ex did that still hurts and angers you. Then capture the first thought that comes to mind after writing the sentence. It may be a feeling or thought that actually contradicts the forgiveness you are trying to express. It may be an emotional rebuttal or protest to what you have just written. Keep writing the "I forgive you for_____" statements for every thought or feeling that comes to the surface.

Your list may fill one page or even two. Don't be discouraged if your angry protests contradict the concept of forgiveness or are so firm and vehement that it seems as if you have not expressed any forgiveness at all. You are in the process of forgiving this person, so keep writing until all the pockets of resentment have been drained. Once again, show this list to no one, but using an empty chair, read the list aloud as though the person were sitting there listening to you.

Here is a sample of what a woman wrote to her former husband, who had divorced her:

Dear Jim,

I forgive you for not being willing to share your feelings with me.	"No, I don't. I still feel cheated by you. You were one way when we dated and then changed as soon as we were married."
I forgive you for withdrawing from me when I wanted to talk about our problems.	"I am still angry over your silence."
I forgive you for not trying to make our marriage work.	"Why couldn't you have tried more? We might have made it!"
I forgive you for sitting around watching TV when I wanted to go out and have fun.	"It's still hard for me to understand why you didn't want to be with me."

| I forgive you for the times you said I was just like your mother. | "I guess there may have been some times when I acted the way she did. If only you had shared that with me earlier." |
| I forgive you for upsetting my life so much with this stupid divorce. | "I have trouble forgiving you for this. I don't think it had to be this way." |

After she identified these as her main hurts, she continued to write these "forgiveness statements" each day for a week until she had no more rebuttals or complaints. When that happens, forgiveness is beginning.

Another way to do this is to take just one of the items you resent and write it again and again on the paper, listing every rebuttal that comes to mind until you can say, "I forgive you for____" several times without any objection coming to mind. This will move you from living in the past to living in the present.

If forgiveness seems elusive at this point, listen to these words of encouragement from Dr. Lloyd John Ogilvie:

> The sure sign that we have an authentic relationship with God is that we believe more in the future than in the past. The past can be neither a source of confidence nor a condemnation. God graciously divided our life into days and years so that we could let go of yesterdays and anticipate our tomorrows. For the past mistakes, He offers forgiveness and an ability to forget. For our tomorrows, He gives us the gift of expectation and excitement.[9]

One of our problems is that most of us have better memories than God does. We cling to our hurts and nurse them, which causes us to experience difficulty with others. We actually play God when we refuse to forgive others or ourselves. When we don't forgive, it not only fractures our relationship with others but with God as well.

Is it fair to be stuck to a painful past? Is it fair to be walloped again and again by the same old hurt? Vengeance is having a videotape planted in your soul that cannot be turned off. It plays the painful scene over and over inside your mind. It hooks you into its instant replays. Each time it replays, you feel the pain again. Is it fair?

Forgiving turns off the videotape of pained memory. Forgiving sets you free. Forgiving is the only way to stop the cycle of unfair pain in your memory.[10]

Perhaps Webster's definition of *forget* can give you some insight into the attitude and response you can choose. *Forget* means "to lose the remembrance of . . . to treat with inattention or disregard . . . to disregard intentionally; overlook; to cease remembering or noticing . . . to fail to become mindful at the proper time." Is there someone in your life who is suffering from emotional malnutrition because of resentment and unforgiveness? Is it you?

Not forgiving means inflicting inner torment upon ourselves. When we reinforce those tormenting messages, we make ourselves miserable and ineffective. Forgiveness is saying, "It is all right, it is over. I no longer resent you or see you as an enemy. I love you, even if you cannot love me back."

When you forgive someone for hurting you, you perform spiritual surgery inside your soul; you cut away the wrong that was done to you so that you can see your "enemy" through the magic eyes that can heal your soul. Detach that person from the hurt and let it go, the way children open their hands and let a trapped butterfly go free.

Then invite that person back into your mind, fresh, as if a piece of history between you had been erased, its grip on your memory broken. Reverse the seemingly irreversible flow of pain within you.[11]

We are able to forgive because God has forgiven us. He has given us a beautiful model of forgiveness. Allowing God's forgiveness to permeate our lives and renew us is the first step toward wholeness.

Lewis Smedes once said in response to the question, "How do you know when you have forgiven a person?" you have forgiven when in your heart you begin to wish that person well. When we can pray for that person and ask for God's blessing upon him or her, we have forgiven. But again, it is gradual and may take months or years to work through the hurt and pain of the breakup.

To finalize your act of forgiveness, it may be helpful to write a statement of release to your ex. The woman described earlier, who was struggling to forgive her ex-husband, is a good example of what can happen in overcoming the hurt of the past. She said in her release statement:

> Dear Jim,
>
> I release you from the responsibility I gave you to determine how I have been feeling because of the divorce. I never did understand all that happened to make you the way you were, and I probably never will. It doesn't matter now. What matters is I release you from the bitterness and resentment I have held toward you over the past three years. I release you from my expectations of who and what you should have been. I forgive you.

Pray for the strength of Jesus Christ in your life as you release your past to Him. Freeing that person through forgiveness gives you freedom as well. And in doing that you are able to experience the abundance that Jesus Christ has for you.

Another step in this process is desensitizing painful places and locations. I have talked to people who have changed jobs, avoided restaurants and what used to be favorite recreational haunts, and even churches because they were painful reminders of what used to be. But this is allowing the other person to control and dominate your life. It is vital that you return to all these places and take control of them. Perhaps you vacationed at some special places before your divorce and you would like to return. But fear holds you back. Take a close friend or relative with you. Give this place to Jesus Christ in your prayers, and ask Him to take the pain away from that place. Go back to the restaurant or church. Make it a special time and ask God's blessing on the location and the occasion. The more you stay away, the greater your fear and aversion. By returning, you dilute the pain.

It is common to write a love letter in the building stage of a relationship. It is uncommon to write one to conclude a relationship, yet this practice can definitely put it to rest. This final love letter is one in which you collect all your thoughts, including anger, pleas, rationalizations, concerns, or apologies. Write it all in a letter, but do not mail it. This project could continue for several days, or it could be a one-time occurrence. It includes setting to rest your unfulfilled dreams with this person and what this individual will be missing out on because of not having you as a part of his or her life. This is a cleansing action, especially when you read the letter aloud to an empty chair, give all the contents to God in prayer, free yourself from the tyranny of these thoughts over you, and say your final good-bye.

Stage Five: Rebuilding and *Stage Six: Resolution.* At these stages, you are finally able to talk about the future with a sense of hope. You have just about completed your detachment from the other person, hopefully without lingering fears. Healthy new attachments may occur at this time.

We need to remember, however, that there are three possible outcomes of a relationship breakup: a change for the better; a change for the worse; or a return to the previous level of living. At the outset of the breakup, it is almost impossible to conceive of things changing for the better, especially if you are the one who was rejected. In the latter stages of the crisis, you may be able to see glimmers of possibility for positive change. Your judgments and decisions during this turning point in your life will make the difference in the outcome.

Notes

Chapter 10 The Loss of a Relationship

1. Lynn Caine, *Widow* (New York: William Morrow and Company, 1974), 97.

2. Anita Brock, *Divorce Recovery* (Fort Worth, Texas: Worthy Publishing, 1988), 20, adapted.

3. Ibid., 19–23, adapted.

4. Dr. Zev Wanderer and Tracy Cabot, *Letting Go* (New York: Dell Publishing, 1978), 27, 28, adapted.

5. Gary Emery, Ph.D., *A New Beginning: How You Can Change Your Thoughts Through Cognitive Therapy* (New York: Simon & Schuster, Inc., 1981, 1988), 61.

6. Wanderer and Cabot, *Letting Go,* 97–100, adapted.

7. Brock, *Divorce Recovery,* 39–45, adapted.

8. Stephen Gullo, Ph.D., and Connie Church, *Love Shock* (New York: Bantam Books, 1988), 97–119, adapted.

9. Lloyd John Ogilvie, *God's Best for My Life* (Eugene, Oregon: Harvest House Publishers, 1981), 1.

10. Lewis B. Smedes, "Forgiveness, the Power to Change the Past," *Christianity Today,* January 7, 1983, 26.

11. Lewis B. Smedes, *Forgive and Forget* (New York: Harper and Row, Publishers, 1984), 37.

11
Helping Others With Their Losses

" "I would like to help. I really would. But I just don't know what to say. I'm sure I say too much, and sometimes I think what I say hurts more than it helps. So, most of the time, I stay away and don't do anything at all."

An uncommon response? No. It is probably the most common feeling of frustration we experience when a friend or loved one is going through a loss. We all struggle with what to say, how to say it, and when to respond. But it is possible to learn how to minister to others in a way that is supportive and caring.

As Christians, we have an opportunity to share Christ's love by the way we reach out to comfort and support others when they have endured a loss. But there are guidelines for us to follow in reacting to the grief of a friend or relative. You will need to acknowledge that the loss has occurred in this person's life and see it through the person's eyes rather than your own.

There are four major "Do Nots" that need to be followed: (1) Do not withdraw from the relative or friend. (2) Do not compare, evaluate, or judge the person or his or her responses. (3) Do not look for sympathy for yourself. (4) Do not patronize or pity the person.

In the case of any loss, a person needs continuing, ongoing support from a number of people. Sometimes the support we give is out of proportion. When there is a death, the bereaved person is often inundated by people, calls, and cards. But two weeks later, the person feels like a social outcast. Nobody calls, nobody writes. It is as though the whole world has gone merrily on its way, leaving the person alone. This creates a tremendous feeling of isolation. The bereaved person needs comfort on a consistent basis. He or she needs to be able to talk over what has occurred and reminisce. In both death and divorce, there are major decisions that need to be made. In all types of loss, a support group may be needed immediately.

When you see your friend or relative, the most basic response is to ask how the person is doing and feeling. The important thing is to let the person talk without comparing, evaluating, or judging. Here are some statements to avoid:

"I don't understand why you're still crying. Life goes on, you know."

"Look, you only lost your stepfather. What about your mother? She has a greater loss than you, and she's pulled herself together."

"No one should feel that way about losing a cat. It's only an animal. You had it for ten years, and you can find another one."

"This will make your family closer. It's an opportunity to grow together."

"I'm sure this will teach the other college students to be more diligent in their studies."

"Don't you appreciate what you have left?"

"Next time we'll be sure not to use that doctor or hospital."

"You've started out in new jobs before, so just look at this layoff as a great opportunity, the way George did when he got fired."

Other statements that too many grievers have had to hear are:

"Don't cry."

"Be brave."

"You'll get over it in a couple of weeks."

"You shouldn't feel that way. After all, you have the Lord."

"It's time to pull yourself together. You wouldn't want Mother seeing you that way, would you?"

"The past needs to be put behind us. Let's move on to the future with God."

"At least he didn't suffer."

"Well, just be glad it wasn't your only child."

"Look at it this way—losing your husband this young and without children will make it easier for you to handle."

"Everyone dies sooner or later. He just died sooner."

"The children need you to be strong."

Statements like these don't help or comfort. They only intensify the person's feelings of loss and despair.

Sometimes people take an "It could have been worse" approach with a grieving friend in the hope of lessening the hurt. Unfortunately, at this point in time it doesn't work. In *The Survival Guide for Widows*, the author describes this approach:

> I have one friend who, whenever we got together, at one point would nod her head wisely and say sententiously, "There are worse things than death." It was home-truth time, and she wanted me to know how lucky I was that I didn't have a living vegetable tied up to tubes in the hospital, or a human skeleton wasting away with pain in front of my eyes. I know, I know. We are given enough strength, I hope, to bear our own pain. I would not trade with others, nor they with me, in all likelihood. . . . But the widow doesn't feel very lucky and resents being reminded that she still owes a debt of gratitude. She'll come around to it.[1]

The third "Do Not" involves eliciting sympathy for yourself. It sounds strange, but it does happen. Some people talk about their own sense of loss and grief in an effort to express sorrow and empathy. But you cannot expect the other person to help you at this time. This is a time for you to give, not receive. If you need assistance, get it from somebody else.

Have you ever felt patronized by another person? You know what that feels like, don't you? You end up feeling dependent and childlike. You begin to wallow in self-pity and feel worse than before you interacted with the "helpful" person. Any kind of condescending response or behavior tends to reinforce the hurt and basically shows that you don't really care as much as you say.

There are several positive guidelines to follow in ministering to a friend, relative, or neighbor. The first step is simply accepting what has happened and how the person is responding. You may have your own perspective on what the person should be doing or how he or she should be responding. Revise your expectations. You are not the other person or an authority on that individual's responses.

Accept grieving people and let them know their feelings are normal. Some of them will apologize to you for their tears, depression, or anger. You will hear comments like these: "I can't believe I'm still crying like this. I'm so sorry." "I don't know why I'm still so upset. It was unfair of them to let me go after fifteen years at that job. I know I shouldn't be angry, but I guess I really am. It seems so unfair."

You can be an encourager by accepting their feelings and the fact that they have feelings. Give them the gift of facing their feelings and expressing them. There are many statements you can make to them:

"I don't want you to worry about crying in front of me. It's hard to feel this sad and not express it in tears. You may find me crying with you at times."

"I hope you feel the freedom to express your sorrow in tears in front of me. I won't be embarrassed or upset. I just want to be here with you.''

''If I didn't see you cry, I would be more concerned. Your crying tells me you are handling this in a healthy way.''

''If I had experienced what you have been through, I would feel like opening my eyes and letting the flood of tears come pouring out. Do you ever feel like that?''

Anger is another feeling that is difficult for many people to express. Use comments like these:

''It is natural to feel anger and hostility toward everyone and everything that had to do with your husband's death. I feel angry too.''

''You must be very angry that your baby has suffered, and you can do nothing about it.''

''It is normal and reasonable to be angry and resentful when you have lost your baby, and others have live and healthy babies.''

''You have lost your daughter and you have a right to be angry and frustrated.''

''It must be hard to find the words to express your anger, helplessness, and frustration.''

''It is important that you allow yourself to express your anger and rage no matter how much others try to discourage you.''[2]

Your encouragement will help grieving persons understand that their expression of feelings will not cause you to withdraw from them. Reassure them that you are not going to leave because of their feelings or try to talk them out of feeling the way they do. Your support is going to remain.

Another positive way of responding is touch. But be sensitive to people you are ministering to who may not be as comfortable with touch as you are. If they seem to reject your physical gestures, such as hugs or touch, be sure to respect them. If you extend a hand on the shoulder and they stiffen up, it is a good indication that your brief words and physical presence will help more than touch. In time, they may come to you and say, "I need a hug."

Sometimes it helps just to say, "I will be here in the home with you for a while. When you need me to leave or to do something for you, please let me know, and I will do it." Never assume that they don't need you. Find out by talking with them.

Many people you minister to *will* need touch, since for many people, touching eases the emptiness of the inner pain. A widow expresses her feelings in this way:

> . . . your mind is still on crutches. . . . There is something awe-inspiring, silencing, and shattering about emotional pain that does leave one at a loss for words. Perhaps gestures are better. I've mentioned before my need for hugs. I'm sure other people feel the same way. Human physical comfort, no strings. I saw a cartoon once, no caption. . . . It was a vending machine; the sign on it read: "Hugs 25 cents." I wish I could have one installed.[3]

In his delightful book *Just a Touch of Nearness*, Fred Bauer tells this story:

> I once heard about the tragic traffic death of a young child. Nancy, just six years old, had been struck by a speeding car. Her parents were devastated. So were her schoolmates, especially Joyce, Nancy's closest friend. As soon as Joyce heard the news about Nancy, she wanted to run to her friend's house. But Joyce's mother thought it would be too upsetting for their daughter and for Nancy's parents. "Daddy and you and I will go to the funeral," she consoled. "You can see Nancy's parents there." But a tearful Joyce insisted that she must see them immediately.

What worried Joyce's mother was what she herself might say to the grieving parents. But finally, reluctantly, she agreed to take her daughter to Nancy's house. And when they arrived, Joyce ran to her lost friend's mother, climbed up on her lap, and threw her arms around her. Wordlessly, the two of them cried out their mutual hurt.

No one who came to say, "I'm sorry," said it better than Joyce.[4]

One of the greatest gifts you can give to a hurting, grieving person is the gift of listening. We are called to be listeners. As James says, "Be a ready listener " (*see* James 1:19 AMPLIFIED).

Listening is a fine art, but it is a gift of spiritual significance you can learn to give to others. In Proverbs we read, "The hearing ear and the seeing eye, the Lord has made both of them" (Proverbs 20:12 AMP). When you listen to others, you give them a sense of importance, hope, and love that they may not receive any other way. Through listening, we nurture and validate the feelings of others, especially when they are experiencing difficulties in life.

Listening is giving sharp attention to what someone else is sharing with you. Notice that I didn't say, "what someone else is *saying* to you." Often what people *share* with us is more than what they say. We must listen to the total person, not just the words he or she speaks. Listening requires openness to whatever is being shared: feelings, attitudes, and concerns as well as words. Listening also means putting yourself in a position to respond to whatever is being shared with you.

Listening is an expression of love. It involves caring enough to take seriously what another person is communicating. When you listen lovingly, you invite that person into your life as a guest.

When people know you hear them, they will trust you and feel safe with you. And if you are a good listener, others will be more apt to invite you into their lives. Those you listen to will also learn through your example to respond openly and lovingly to what you share with them.

Since the Word of God calls each believer to be a ready listener, we must understand what it means to listen. There is a difference between listening and hearing. Hearing is basically to gain content or information for your own purposes. In hearing, you are concerned about what is going on inside *you* during the conversation. You are tuned in to your own reactions, responses, thoughts, and feelings.

Listening means caring for and empathizing with the person you are listening to. In listening, you are trying to understand the thoughts and feelings of the speaker. You are listening for the person's sake, not your own. You are not thinking about what you are going to say when the speaker stops talking. You are not engrossed in formulating your own response. You are concentrating on what is being said.

Nurturing listening is very important in helping others. In this type of listening, you listen for the emotional content behind the message being shared and reflect it to the speaker in an empathetic manner in your own words. Nurturing listening conveys support, caring, and acceptance for the person and his or her point of view. It extends a warm invitation to the griever to share deepest joys, concerns, or hurts with you.

The following dialogue, one of the weekly telephone conversations between Frank and his father, illustrates nurturing listening. Frank's father and mother had been married for fifty-one years before she died nearly three years ago. Frank's father was deeply shaken by his loss and he still doesn't go out much. Many of his friends have encouraged him to continue his hobbies and to stay busy visiting his many grandchildren. Notice how Frank nurtures his father by simply listening and sharing empathetic responses:

> Frank: Hi, Dad. How are you doing today?
> Dad: I'm getting along just fine, son.

Frank: You're doing okay, then.

Dad: Yes, as well as I can with your mother gone.

Frank: Dad, it sounds as if you still feel Mom's passing deeply. It was a real loss.

Dad: You know, I didn't think it was going to be this bad. I didn't think it would take this long to recover.

Frank: After all the years you were together, you miss her and miss the times you had together.

Dad (after a pause, with a slight break in his voice): Frank, I miss her each day, and sometimes I feel lonely all day long. Lots of friends want me to move on with life and not think about her so much. But I want to remember. There are so many good memories.

Frank: You sound as if you want to do something to help you remember Mom.

Dad: This may sound dumb, but I really want to go visit some of the places Mom and I used to go together. I was thinking about taking one or two of the grandkids with me. What do you think?[5]

Did Frank give his opinion of what his father ought to do? Did he advise his father on a decision? Did he try to cheer up his father? No. He simply listened reflectively in a way that nurtured his father and encouraged him to express his inner thoughts and feelings. Frank's responses made his dad feel understood. That's what people want: someone who understands and accepts them. As you learn to nurture others with your listening, you can fill their need for understanding and acceptance.

As you listen, you are going to hear the same expression of feelings again and again. Grieving people, whether it is the loss of a pet, a job, a home, or a person, have a compelling need to retell the details of their loss. They want to talk about the who, what, when, and how. The details vary, depending upon the nature of the loss. Do you remember why people tend to focus so much upon the details and, in some cases, final conversations with someone they lost? It gives them an opportunity to hold on to whatever they lost. Don't be put off by the details of the story, even though you may know them by heart. This telling of details goes on for three or four months until they are assured they will not lose the memory of the person they lost. When they reach that point, the clinging to exacting details will lessen. They will begin to let go.

When grieving people give the details, encourage them to tell about accompanying feelings as well. Their feelings will be relieved as you listen without shock, embarrassment, or judgment.

Often in cases of accidents, loss of important positions, or death, you will hear people taking responsibility for what occurred, even when they had no responsibility and could not do anything about what happened. This is an opportunity for you to say something like:

"What could you have done to prevent that from happening? Would that really have been possible? Is there anyone else who could have done anything? If so, why didn't they? I can see how you might feel that way, but there really was nothing any of us could have done." Before you make statements such as these, help them identify all of their "if only" and "regret" statements that were discussed earlier in this book.

Above all, don't say too much to the hurting person. Your presence speaks volumes. Joe Bayly wrote a book many years ago called *Last Thing We Talk About* (formerly titled *The View From the Hearse*). It is the story of how he and his wife coped with the deaths of three of their sons. He gave this advice:

> Sensitivity in the presence of grief should usually make us more silent, more listening. "I'm sorry" is honest; "I know how you feel" is usually not—even though you may have experienced the death of a person who had the same familial relationship to you as the deceased person had to

the grieving one. If the person feels that you can understand, he'll tell you. Then you may want to share your own honest, not prettied-up feelings in your personal aftermath with death. Don't try to "prove" anything to a survivor. An arm around the shoulder, a firm grip of the hand, a kiss: these are the proofs grief needs, not logical reasoning. I was sitting, torn by grief. Someone came and talked to me of God's dealings, of why it happened, of hope beyond the grave. He talked constantly, he said things I knew were true. I was unmoved, except to wish he'd go away. He finally did. Another came and sat beside me. He didn't ask leading questions. He just sat beside me for an hour and more, listened when I said something, answered briefly, prayed simply, left. I was moved. I was comforted. I hated to see him go.[6]

If you find yourself struggling with what to say, the written note or card is a wonderful way to comfort a griever. I have saved many of the written expressions we received after the loss of our son. They did two things for me: I was comforted and felt loved by those who wrote. Their expressions assisted me with my own expression of grief, for I felt the loss more sharply each time I read a note. You can send personal words of comfort, quotes, poems, and the Word of God. Scriptures such as the following are helpful:

> The eternal God is your Refuge, And underneath are the everlasting arms.
>
> Deuteronomy 33:27 TLB

> When you go through deep waters and great trouble, I will be with you. When you go through rivers of difficulty, you will not drown! When you walk through the fire of oppression, you will not be burned up—the flames will not

consume you. For I am the Lord your God, your Savior, the Holy One of Israel. . . . Don't be afraid, for I am with you.

Isaiah 43:2, 3, 5 TLB

Let not your heart be troubled: ye believe in God. . . .

John 14:1 KJV

For I am persuaded, that neither death, nor life, nor angels, nor principalities, nor powers, nor things present, nor things to come, Nor height, nor depth, nor any other creature, shall be able to separate us from the love of God, which is in Christ Jesus our Lord.

Romans 8:38, 39 KJV

Even though I walk through the valley of the shadow of death, I fear no evil; for Thou art with me; Thy rod and Thy staff, they comfort me.

Psalms 23:4 NAS

God is our refuge and strength, a very present help in trouble.

Psalms 46:1 KJV

He heals the brokenhearted . . . .

Psalms 147:3 RSV

. . . he hath said, I will never leave thee, nor forsake thee.

Hebrews 13:5 KJV

. . . hope we have as an anchor of the soul, both sure and steadfast. . . .

Hebrews 6:19 KJV

Let not your hearts be troubled; believe in God. . . .

John 14:1 RSV

Fear not, for I am with you, be not dismayed, for I am your God; I will strengthen you, I will help you, I will uphold you. . . .

Isaiah 41:10 RSV

The eternal God is thy refuge, and underneath are the everlasting arms.

Deuteronomy 33:27 KJV

Trust in the Lord with all thine heart; and lean not unto thine own understanding. In all thy ways acknowledge him, and he shall direct thy paths.

Proverbs 3:5, 6 KJV

When I pray, you answer me, and encourage me by giving me the strength I need.

Psalms 138:3 TLB

Be strong and of a good courage, fear not . . . for the Lord thy God, he it is that doth go with thee; he will not fail thee, nor forsake thee.

Deuteronomy 31:6 KJV

There are many poems you can use. Helen Steiner Rice has written some of the most meaningful ones. Her books can be found in most libraries and Christian bookstores.

Personal notes which include quotes, selected with sensitivity and the specific person in mind, take a little extra time and thought, but the healing effect they may have on a grief-stricken friend is well worth the effort. Sources for short, comforting quotes are almost limitless. One delightful little book, full of words of wisdom that will turn weakness into strength, is *When Sorrow Comes*. Here is a passage from that book that I have shared with those in despair:

I wish I had a magic word to wipe away your tears! I do not know any magic words, but I know a God who can heal you and I commend Him to you. Remember, the door of death is the only door that leads to the Father's house. He will be waiting there to greet and welcome His children.

Peter Marshall, the legendary Scottish chaplain of the United States Senate in the late 1940s, died at age forty-six. Uncanny as it seems, he was reported to have spoken words befitting his own eulogy: "The measure of a life, after all, is not its duration, but its donation." When the death of a younger person occurs, these words may be appropriately incorporated into a personal note.

Quotes included in notes do not have to be spoken by famous people. The main criterion is that the quote is something that helps soothe the hurt caused by the death of a loved one.[7]

The prayers of others are helpful to share at the death of a loved one. In the book *Wonderful Promises,* there is a prayer that says:

Lord, when sometimes my life in this world seems too much to bear, help me to claim Your wonderful promise of victory over tears, death, sorrow and pain. I thank you that all things are made new through You and that I will share in Your kingdom.[8]

Another prayer that can help a person face feelings is the following:

I am empty, Father, I am bitter, even toward You. I grieve, not only for the one I have lost, but for the loving part of myself that seems to have died as well. You, who have at other times brought the dead back to life, revive my dead ability to live, to be close, to care about this world and those I know. I believe, I insist, that You can heal this mortal wound.[9]

If there is one character quality that is necessary in ministering to a grieving person, it is patience. You will hear the same story, the same details, the same tears again and again. This is normal and necessary. What may be quite uncomfortable for you is anger. The extent of the person's anger may cause you to want to say, ''Enough!'' But it is a natural, healthy response if it is within reasonable bounds.

You may even become the target for the person's anger. If he or she withdraws, don't push him. This is part of grief. It is as though he moves in and out of the real world. He will progress at his pace, not yours. The author of *Beyond Grief* describes the process so well:

> No schedule exists for healing. A survivor is raw with grief and must endure much pain before healing takes place. The only course you can take is to avoid appearing restless or annoyed with the survivor.
>
> It may be difficult for you to achieve a balance between *acknowledging the loss* that caused the survivor pain, and *maintaining a positive perspective* in the face of that loss. You cannot help the survivor by blocking reality or steering a survivor away from painful reminders of the loss, but at the same time, you need to maintain a positive perspective while facilitating grief.
>
> You can do this by validating the person who died, talking about how the person touched or enriched the lives of other people. When the opportunity arises, mention facts of life in which the survivor has formerly shown interest. Make a mental list of those activities or people who gave the survivor enjoyment. Keep the sparks of those natural interests alive or at least present, by mentioning them—the garden, the pets, the survivor's favorite shopping area, golf partner, or community interest. By doing this you are indicating to the survivor that *there has been a past* and *there will be a future* with these same things, people, and places in it.[10]

There are also many practical things you can do to help, regardless of the type of loss. I hope you will begin to respond to all of the losses people experience, some of which don't have much social recognition or support. Any major loss cuts very deep, whether it is divorce, personal rejection, job loss, or death.

With each loss you will need to (1) discover the grieving person's personal situation and needs; (2) decide what you are willing and able to do for the person, realizing that you can't do it all, nor should you, and finally (3) contact the person and offer to do the most difficult of the jobs you have chosen. If the person rejects your offer, suggest another. Specific tasks could include feeding pets, making or delivering meals, yard work, making difficult phone calls, obtaining needed information regarding support groups or new employment, providing transportation, being available to run errands, and so forth. At some point in time, giving the person a sensitive, supportive book on loss and grief could be helpful.[11]

If the loss affected one person, minister to that person. But if it affected the family unit, there needs to be a ministry to each family member, both adults and children. Discover which of their social involvements will be the most difficult for them and be available for support.

As each year goes by, friends and relatives lose loved ones. Prior to Christmas, we look over the Christmas card list to make sure we have made the proper changes so the name on the card doesn't upset the recipient. For a widow, receiving cards still addressed to "Mr. and Mrs." can be painful.

Someone, whether it is you or another concerned individual, will need to help the grieving individual(s) accomplish several tasks. These tasks are especially applicable in the loss of a loved one and will be accomplished over a period of time.

Help grieving people identify secondary losses and resolve any unfinished business with the lost person. For many, these losses are never identified or grieved over. It could be the loss of a role, the family unit, the breadwinner, social life, and so on. Sometimes saying aloud what a grieving person never said or had an opportunity to say to the deceased helps to complete some of the unfinished business.

Help them recognize that in addition to grieving for the lost person, grief will need to be experienced for any dreams, expectations, or fantasies they had for the person. This is sometimes difficult or even overlooked, since they are not usually seen as losses because they never existed. Yet each still constitutes a loss because these dreams have a high value.

Discover what the grieving persons are capable of doing and where they might be lacking in their coping skills. Help them handle the areas where they are struggling. Encourage positive things they are doing such as talking about the loss. When they do something unhealthy, such as avoidance, alcohol, or overmedication, give them other alternatives.

Since most people do not understand the duration and process of grieving, provide them with helpful information concerning what they are now experiencing. You want to normalize their grief without minimizing it. But also let them know that their grief responses will be unique, and they should avoid comparing themselves with anyone else. Don't let them equate the length and amount of grieving with how much they loved the person.

Let them know you understand they may want to avoid the intensity of the pain they are presently experiencing. Your empathy, understanding, and respect will do much to assist them in knowing that their grief is normal. Encourage them to go through the pain of the grief. There is just no way to avoid it. If they do, it will explode at some other time. They may need reminding that even with the present intensity of their pain, in time it will diminish.

Help them understand that their grief will affect all areas of life. Work habits, memory, attention span, intensity of feelings, and response to a marital partner will all be affected. This is normal.

Help them understand the process of grief. Sharing one of the charts in this book may be helpful at the appropriate time. Understanding that their emotions will vary and that progress is erratic will help alleviate the feeling that there is no progress. Help them plan for significant dates and holidays in advance. Encourage them to talk about their expectations for themselves and help them evaluate whether or not they are being realistic.

Help them find ways to be replenished spiritually, socially, and physically. Be aware of their eating and exercise habits. Don't let them forego their own regular checkups. Alert them to the possible diminished capacity of the immune system that occurs several months after a major loss.

Help them with the practical problems following a loss, and assist in preventing unwise decisions. Such practical items as helping to arrange for meals, transportation, financial consultation, or eventually training or education needed for survival may be part of your task.

Sometimes grieving people will make major decisions too early, which creates additional losses. Some plan to sell their houses or move to new cities, but this may eliminate their roots or a needed support system. Making major changes during the first year should be discouraged if at all possible. These changes may appear to be wise, but they also bring another sense of loss.

Over a longer period of time, there will be a number of tasks with which you may be able to assist grieving persons. These have been covered in earlier portions of this book, but let's go over them again briefly.

Help them discover their new identity separate from the one they lost and what new roles they must either develop or relinquish. These changes must be identified so that even such things as lost portions of identity (from married to single) and lost roles can be grieved for.

You may be the one to bring up the fact that a healthy new relationship with the lost person must be developed. You may even want to read portions of this book with them and discuss what has been read. This thought will be foreign to many, but it is a major adjustment for everyone who has lost a loved one. It is helpful to ask them how they plan to keep parts of their former life alive, such as special times, routines, or mementos, and how reminiscing can be helpful.

One of your future tasks will be helping grieving persons reinvest in new lives. They will be able to start this process at their own time and pace. Some will need direction in getting back into the mainstream of life, especially if they cared for a chronically ill person for a period of time, or even if they placed an elderly or handicapped person in a home. There can be a tremendous sense of loss and resulting adjustment to life following this step. Sometimes finding support groups or other means of social support will end up providing lasting relationships. You need to be sensitive to the ability and desire of people to get back into the mainstream of life. Be sure you don't encourage them into new relationships too soon. Be especially careful of trying to promote new dating activities for those who have lost spouses through death or divorce.

At some point in time, you will have the opportunity to talk with people about what they have learned through a loss experience. In any kind of loss, there can be growth and gain, but this is not seen immediately. This does not mean we deny the significance of the loss in any way, but we do come to the place where our loss becomes an opportunity for spiritual growth and learning.[12]

In deciding how you can minister to others, you will find a set of helpful guidelines in *What to Say When You Don't Know What to Say* by Lauren Briggs. I would encourage you to read it over again and again so it will truly be yours when you need to reach out and minister to another person.

Guidelines to Help Others

What it's best not to do:

Don't try to minimize their pain with comments like,
"It's probably for the best." "Things could be worse."
"You'll remarry." "You're young; you can always have
another one." "You're strong; you'll get over it soon."
"You know God is in control." Comments like these might
be an attempt to offer hope, but to a hurting person, they
sound as if you don't comprehend the enormity of what has
happened. These statements don't acknowledge pain and
loss.

What it's best to do:

You can offer simple, understanding statements such as,
"I feel for you during this difficult time." "This must be
very hard for you." "I share your feelings of loss." "I
wish I could take the hurt away." Comments like these let
the people know you acknowledge their pain and it is okay
for them to feel that way.

What it's best not to do:

Don't say "I'm so sorry" and end the sentence. Your
hurting friend is probably sorry too, but he can't respond to
that kind of comment.

What it's best to do:

Say, "I'm so sorry." Then add, "I know how special he
was to you." "I'll miss her also." "I want to help you; I'm
available anytime you need me." "I've been praying for
you. Is there something specific I should be praying for?"

What it's best not to do:

> Don't just say, "Is there anything I can do to help?"

What it's best to do:

> Be aggressive with your willingness to help. Ask yourself, *What would I need if I were in a similar situation?* Offer specific things you can do for them: "I'm on my way to the store. What can I pick up for you?" "Would tomorrow be a good day to help you with the laundry?" "Would the children like to come over and play this afternoon?" Most of the time, people in a crisis can't decide what they do need. Besides, they probably don't want to impose.

What it's best not to do:

> Don't say, "You shouldn't feel that way."

What it's best to do:

> Encourage them to keep a journal or write down their thoughts and feelings. Often, just seeing their thoughts on paper helps them deal with what they are facing.

What it's best not to do:

> Do not try to answer when they ask, "Why?" You don't have any answer, and at this time even the true answer may not be apparent. Job's friends didn't help with their responses and Job said, "Miserable comforters are you all!" (Job 16:2 NIV).

What it's best to do:

> Simply answer, "I don't know why. I guess both of us would like to have some answers at this time. You would especially. I wish I had an answer to give you."

What it's best not to do:

Don't offer spiritual answers as to why they are facing this problem or tell them they'll be stronger afterward. We don't know why tragedies happen and why certain people have to go through such trauma. We do our friends a disservice by offering possible explanations.

What it's best to do:

Agree when individuals express their feelings. Say, "Yes, what happened to you isn't fair and doesn't make any sense," whether or not you share the same perspective.

What it's best not to do:

Don't put the recovery of hurting friends on timetables. Your inference that they are not coping well or should be their old selves by now only hinders their progress. Everyone is different, and recovery varies.

What it's best to do:

Allow them all the time they need to deal effectively with all the phases of their grief.

What it's best not to do:

Don't quote Bible verses as a way to correct or minimize their feelings. Think very carefully, asking yourself if a passage will communicate comfort or condemnation. Never offer spiritual suggestions from a position of superiority or self-righteousness.

What it's best to do:

Give spiritual encouragement from your heart, and include Bible verses that have comforted you at a difficult time. Let them know you will pray for them daily. If you pray with them, keep it brief, reflecting their feelings in the prayer and focusing upon God's understanding of their pain and the fact that He will be their Source of comfort.

What it's best not to do:

Don't say "I understand" when you haven't faced the same situation. Telling people that everything will be all right when you have never known the depth of their hardship is an empty statement. And they don't need to hear horror stories of people you know who have been through something similar.

What it's best to do:

Be honest about your experiences. If you haven't endured their particular kind of tragedy, say, "I haven't been through what you're facing, but I want you to know I care about you and will support you through the difficult time ahead." If you've had a similar crisis, tell about it briefly, adding that you can empathize with their feelings. Of course, you can't completely understand because you haven't been through the past experiences that laid the foundation for their reaction.

What it's best not to do:

Don't ignore their needs after the immediate loss has subsided.

What it's best to do:

Keep in touch for months, especially at the critical times discussed in this book, letting them know you're praying for them. Ask how they are *really* doing, and send thoughtful notes with encouraging words.

What it's best not to do:

Don't expect unrealistic optimism or levity from hurting persons.

What it's best to do:

Realize that their hearts are full of pain and turmoil. Let them know you will listen to their feelings and want to be part of that pain.

What it's best not to do:

Don't offer clichés or be vainly optimistic to cover up your insecurities.

What it's best to do:

Indicate your love by saying, "I really feel awkward because I'm not sure what to say, what you need, or how to help you, but I want you to know that I love you. I'm praying for you and I'm available."

What it's best not to do:

Don't use "shoulds" or "if onlys" such as "You should give the clothes away." "You should go back to work and get over this." "You should have more faith." "If only you had watched him more carefully." "If only you hadn't been so strict." "If only you ate better."

What it's best to do:

Allow hurting people to make the decisions and take the necessary steps to deal with the trauma. No one can tell another person what to feel or not feel.

What it's best not to do:

> Don't offer unasked-for advice. If they weren't solicited, your suggestions may not be appreciated.

What it's best to do:

> Respond cautiously and prayerfully with uplifting and edifying ideas when your friends ask for your help in their tragedy. Let them know that you pray for them daily. On occasion, ask how they would like you to be praying for them.[13]

As you have walked through your own losses, you will be better able to help others walk through their valleys of loss. The walk can be so lonely when it is undertaken alone. But when others come along to just be there, listen, weep, and comfort through their presence, grievers are sustained.

None of us walks alone. Jesus Christ has been there and He is with us all of the time to sustain, encourage, and support us. Yes, life is full of losses, but Jesus Christ makes it possible to conquer them.

Notes

Chapter 11 Helping Others With Their Losses

1. Betty Jane Wylie, *The Survival Guide for Widows* (New York: Ballantine Books, 1982), 115.

2. Donna and Rodger Ewy, *Death of a Dream* (New York: E. P. Dutton, 1984), 80, adapted.

3. Wylie, *Survival Guide for Widows*, 113.

4. Fred Bauer, *Just a Touch of Nearness* (Norwalk, Connecticut: The C. R. Gibson Co., 1985), 24, 25.

5. Source unknown.

6. Joe Bayly, *Last Thing We Talk About* (formerly titled *The View From the Hearse*) (Elgin, Illinois: David C. Cook Publishing Co., 1969), 40.

7. Barbara Russell Chesser, *Because You Care* (Waco, Texas: Word Books, 1987), 122, 123. *When Sorrow Comes* by Robert V. Ozment published by Word Books, 1970.

8. Norman Vincent Peale, *Wonderful Promises* (Carmel, New York: Guideposts, 1983), 32.

9. Phyllis Hobe, *Coping* (Carmel, New York: Guideposts, 1983), 233.

10. Carol Staudacher, *Beyond Grief* (Oakland, California: New Harbinger Publications, 1987), 230, 231.

11. Ibid., 231, 232, adapted.

12. Therese A. Rando, *Grieving: How to Go On Living When Someone You Love Dies* (Lexington, Massachusetts: Lexington Books, 1988), 227–250, adapted.

13. Lauren Briggs, *What You Can Say . . . When You Don't Know What to Say* (Eugene, Oregon: Harvest House Publishers, 1985), 150–155, adapted.

Study Questions

The following study questions can be used by individuals or for group discussion and will help readers apply the suggestions in this book to their own lives.

Chapter 1 The Losses of Life

1. Can you think of a loss in your life that you didn't experience as a loss at the time it happened?

2. Can you describe a loss in your life that you've never fully grieved over? If so, how has this affected you?

3. What experience in your life can you describe as both a gain and a loss?

4. What are two threatened losses that you have experienced in your life that never materialized? How did you feel during the threat? How did you feel after the threat was over?

5. Have you experienced a loss that is not usually described as a loss? Describe it.

6. a. What major loss can you remember experiencing during your teenage years? Describe it.

   b. What is the worst loss you have ever experienced?

c. What do you think are four of the most significant losses men experience?

d. What do you think are four of the most significant losses women experience?

Chapter 2 Losses We Never Considered

Listed below are a series of statements concerning grief and loss. Read each one and then indicate whether you agree or disagree with the statement. After each person in your group has had an opportunity to respond to the questions, indicate by a show of hands who agreed with the statement and who disagreed. Then share with one another why you responded to the statement the way you did. As you proceed through the book, you will develop greater insight into these statements.

1. Grieving is more difficult when people "give in" to their sorrow. Agree_____ Disagree_____

2. Time will eventually heal all wounds or losses. Agree_____ Disagree_____

3. A mature Christian will not grieve over a loss for as long a time as a nonbeliever. Agree_____ Disagree_____

4. There are some people who do not need to grieve, even after a serious loss. Agree_____ Disagree_____

5. The pain of your loss may be just as intense a year later as during the initial few days after the loss occurs. Agree_____ Disagree_____

6. A Christian is not as likely to get as angry at God over a loss as a nonbeliever. Agree_____ Disagree_____

7. It is best to replace something lost as soon as possible in order to help the grieving process. Agree_____ Disagree_____

8. There are some losses in life that are more difficult to handle than the death of a loved one. Agree_____ Disagree_____

9. Asking the question "Why?" during a loss is a reflection of the depth of a person's faith. Agree_____ Disagree_____

10. A person's belief system or theology will affect the way in which he grieves. Agree_____ Disagree_____

11. Grieving for more than a year is abnormal. Agree_____ Disagree_____

12. All suffering we experience in life is God's will for us. Agree_____ Disagree_____

13. There is a healthy aspect to denial when a loss is severe. Agree_____ Disagree_____

Chapter 3 The Meaning of Grief

1. Respond to this list of sentence completion statements by giving your initial response to each one. There are no right or wrong answers, but this is an opportunity for you to identify and share your feelings and beliefs.

To me, grief means . . .

The most difficult part of grieving is . . .

The most intense grief I've ever experienced is . . .

When I experience grief, I feel . . .

The hardest emotion of grief is . . .

What I've never fully grieved for is . . .

The first grief I ever experienced was . . .

What helps me the most when I am grieving is . . .

To me, tears are . . .

My grief usually lasts . . .

2. Would it be helpful for you to write a letter to give to others that would help them better respond to you and your loss? What would you like to say? Perhaps you can begin your letter now and complete it over the next few days. You may want to bring your letters with you for your next session and share them with one another.

Chapter 4 Problems in Grieving and Recovery

1. If you have experienced any of the following, briefly describe:
   a. inhibited grief
   b. delayed grief
   c. conflicted grief
   d. displaced grief
   e. chronic grief
   f. abbreviated grief
   g. replaced grief

   What do you think caused this grief to occur?

   How did the experience affect your physical and emotional health?

   How did you move ahead in your grief recovery?

2. What is the last memory that you have of the most recent loss in your life?

3. On pages 71 and 72 there is a listing of sixteen symptoms of unresolved grief. Do you find yourself experiencing any of these at the present time?

   What can you do about this now?

Chapter 5 Adjusting to the Separation and Void

1. In what way do you need to build a new identity because of your most recent loss?

2. Refer back to the graph on page 84. Using the space provided construct your own listing of both positive and negative events and experiences.

•——•

3. Write a brief paragraph for each event and identify any "regrets" or "if onlys" that you may still experience.

4. Describe some healthy ways that you can relate to your loss.

Chapter 6 Saying Good-bye

1. Identify what you have said good-bye to in your life.

2. How did you say good-bye?

3. Is there someone or something that you need to say good-bye to at this time in your life?

4. Write a good-bye letter to someone or something that you have lost in your life and share it with another person in your group. Describe what this experience meant to you.

Chapter 7 Recovering From Loss

1. Read Psalm 30. Write down what this passage of Scripture is saying to you personally.

2. Rate yourself and your stage in grieving by responding to the evaluation on pages 115–18, and the chart on page 121.

3. Have you ever kept any kind of a journal? How did this help you?

4. What are your questions, fears or concerns about keeping a personal journal?

5. What passages of Scripture have been most helpful to you in your recovery from loss?

Chapter 8 Growing Through Our Losses

1. What are the questions you have raised about God or to God during your loss experience?
2. Read the following passages from the Book of Romans and then respond to the following questions.

For I reckon that the sufferings of this present time are not worthy to be compared with the glory which shall be revealed in us.

For the earnest expectation of the creature waiteth for the manifestation of the sons of God.

For the creature was made subject to vanity, not willingly, but by reason of him who hath subjected the same in hope,

Because the creature itself also shall be delivered from the bondage of corruption into the glorious liberty of the children of God.

For we know that the whole creation groaneth and travaileth in pain together until now.

And not only they, but ourselves also, which have the firstfruits of the Spirit, even we ourselves groan within ourselves, waiting for the adoption, to wit, the redemption of our body.

For we are saved by hope: but hope that is seen is not hope: for what a man seeth, why doth he yet hope for?

But if we hope for that we see not, then do we with patience wait for it (Romans 8:18–25 kjv).

What shall we then say to these things? If God be for us, who can be against us?

He that spared not his own Son, but delivered him up for us all, how shall he not with him also freely give us all things?

Who shall lay any thing to the charge of God's elect? It is God that justifieth.

Who is he that condemneth? It is Christ that died, yea rather, that is risen again, who is even at the right hand of God, who also maketh intercession for us.

Who shall separate us from the love of Christ? shall tribulation, or distress, or persecution, or famine, or nakedness, or peril, or sword?

As it is written, For thy sake we are killed all the day long; we are accounted as sheep for the slaughter.

Nay, in all these things we are more than conquerors through him that loved us.

For I am persuaded, that neither death, nor life, nor angels, nor principalities, nor powers, nor things present, nor things to come,

Nor height, nor depth, nor any other creature, shall be able to separate us from the love of God, which is in Christ Jesus our Lord (Romans 8:31–39 KJV).

    a. What is Paul saying about problems and suffering in life?

    b. What are the reasons for hope as found in this passage?

    c. What are the attributes of God as expressed in this passage?

3. How has worship been a part of your grief recovery? What has made it more difficult to worship at this time?

4. On a scale of 0–10 how close are you now to experiencing James 1:2–3?

5. What can you learn from your most recent loss, or what would you like to learn?

How can you grow because of this loss experience, or how would you like to grow?

How can what you experienced be used for God's glory?

Chapter 9 The Loss of Identity: Who Am I?

1. List three things that you realize you have built your identity on.

2. How have the losses of your life impacted your identity?

3. Evaluate yourself on a scale of 0–10 on the six scales provided for you on pages 144–47. What do your answers tell you about your identity and its source?

   How could you better build your identity at this time in your life?

4. What are some of the dreams that you have given up in the past?

   How has this affected your identity?

Chapter 10 The Loss of a Relationship

1. Reflect back to the first loss that you experienced in a relationship. How did this affect future relationships?

2. What fears do you experience over relationships at the present time?

3. Describe a time in your life you experienced a rejection. Who comforted you at that time?

   How did God comfort you?

4. Is there a person in your life that you still need to forgive? Who?

   Is there anyone in your life who needs to forgive you?

5. Is there an unresolved broken relationship in your life?

If so, what are the steps that you could take to bring closure to that situation? Would the following help?

a. Writing an unmailed angry letter to the person and reading it aloud to God or a good friend?
b. Writing a good-bye letter to this person and reading it aloud.
c. Writing an "I forgive you letter" as described on pages 172–74.
d. Praying for the person and asking God's blessing on him.

6. How will the following verses help you at this time in your life? Isaiah 26:3, Eph. 4:23, Col. 3:1, 2, 2 Cor. 10:5, Phil. 4:6–9.

Chapter 11 Helping Others With Their Losses

1. What are some statements that others have said to you that you wished had never been said?

2. What have been the most helpful words or gestures that others have shared with you?

3. What helpful words would you like others to say to you at the present time?

4. Who is a person that needs you to minister to him or her at the present time?

   What could you say to him or her, and what could you do for him or her?

Describe how you will pray for that person and what passages of Scripture you could share that would be helpful.

5. On pages 198–203 there is a list of what is best "not to do" and what is best "to do." Add to this list your own suggestions for each category.

Bibliography and Other Recommended Resources

Grief

Baker, Don. *Pain's Hidden Purpose.* Portland, Ore.: Multnomah, 1984.

Carlson, Dwight. *When Life Isn't Fair.* Eugene, Ore.: Harvest House, 1989.

Deits, Bob. *Life after Loss.* Tucson: Fisher Books, 1988.

Exley, Richard. *The Rhythm of Life.* Tulsa: Honor Books, 1987.

Greeson, Charlotte, Mary Hollingsworth, and Michael Washburn. *The Grief Adjustment Guide.* Sisters, Ore.: Questar Publishers, 1990.

Jackson, Edgar N. *When Someone Dies.* Philadelphia: Fortress Press, n.d.

Killinger, John. *For God's Sake—Be Human.* Waco: Word, 1970.

Lewis, C. S. *The Problem of Pain,* London: Collins, 1961.

Miller, William. *When Going to Pieces Holds You Together.* Minneapolis: Augsburg, n.d.

Mitchell, Kenneth R., and Herbert Anderson. *All Our Losses, All Our Griefs.* Philadelphia: Westminster Press, 1983.

Ramsay, Dr. Ronald W., and Rene Noorbergen. *Living with Loss.* New York: William Morrow, 1981.

Rando, Therese A. *Grieving: How to Go On Living When Someone You Love Dies.* Lexington, Mass.: Lexington Books, 1988.

————. *Grief, Dying, and Death: Clinical Interventions for Caregivers.* Champaign, Ill.: Research Press, 1984.

Ryan, Dale, and Juanita Ryan. *Recovery from Loss.* Downers Grove, Ill.: InterVarsity Press, 1990.

Simundson, Daniel. *Where Is God in My Suffering?* Minneapolis: Augsburg, 1983.

Singer, Lilly, Margaret Sirot, and Susan Rodd. *Beyond Loss.* New York: E. P. Dutton, 1988.

Stearns, Ann Kaiser. *Living through Personal Crisis.* New York: Ballantine Books, 1984.

Sullender, R. Scott. *Losses in Later Life.* New York: Paulist Press, 1989.

———. *Grief and Growth.* New York: Paulist Press, 1985.

Parent's Death

Krementz, Jill. *How It Feels When a Parent Dies.* New York: Random House, n.d.

Le Shan, Eda. *Learning to Say Goodbye When a Parent Dies.* New York: Macmillan, n.d.

Books for Children

Hammond, Janice M. *When My Dad Died.* Ann Arbor, Mich.: Cranbrook Publishing, n.d.

———. *When My Mommy Died.* Ann Arbor, Mich.: Cranbrook Publishing, n.d.

Death of a Baby

Church, Martha Jo, Helene Chazin, and Faith Ewald. *When a Baby Dies.* The Compassionate Friends, P. O. Box 3696, Oak Brook, IL 60522-3696.

DeFrain, John D., Leona Martens, and Jan and Waren Stork. *Stillborn—The Invisible Death.* Lexington, Mass.: D. C. Heath & Company, Lexington Books, 1986.

Sherokee, Ilse. *Empty Arms—Coping after Miscarriage, Stillbirth and Infant Death.* Available from The Compassionate Friends (address above).

Vredevelt, Pam W. *Empty Arms.* Portland, Ore.: Multnomah, 1984.

Sudden Infant Death Syndrome

DeFrain, John, Jaque Tayloer, and Linda Ernst. *Coping with Sudden Infant Death.* Lexington, Mass.: Lexington Books, 1982.

Schatz, Bill. *Healing a Father's Grief.* Available from The Compassionate Friends (address above).

Stevenson, Nancy, and Cary Straffon. *When Your Child Dies: Finding the Meaning in Mourning.* Available from The Compassionate Friends (address above).

Abducted or Murdered Children

Schiff, Harriet Sarnoff. *The Bereaved Parent*. New York: Penguin Books, 1978.

For Parents: Talking to Children about Death

Dodd, Robert V. *Helping Children Cope with Death*. Scottdale, Pa.: Herald Press, 1984.

Grollman, Earl A. *Talking about Death—A Dialogue between Parent and Child*. Boston: Beacon Press, 1976.

Jewett, Claudia L. *Helping Children Cope with Separation and Loss*. Cambridge: Harvard Common Press, 1982.

For Children Ages 3–7

Alex, Marlee, and Ben Alex. *Grandpa and Me—We Learn about Death*. Minneapolis: Bethany, 1982.

Sanford, Doris. *It Must Hurt a Lot*. Portland, Ore.: Multnomah, 1985.

For Children Ages 8–14

Beckmann, Beverly Ann. *From*. St. Louis: Concordia Publishing House, 1980.

Forral, Marie, and Anders Forral. *Rebecca, a Look at Death*. Minneapolis: Lerner Publications, 1978.

Sims, Alicia. *Am I Still a Sister?* Available from The Compassionate Friends (address above).

Adoption

Zimmerman, Martha. *Should I Keep My Baby?* Minneapolis: Bethany, 1983.

Abortion

Garton, Jean Staker. *Who Broke the Baby?* Minneapolis: Bethany, 1979.

Hanes, Mari, with Jack Hayford. *Beyond Heartache*. Wheaton: Tyndale, 1984.

Linn, Dennis, Matthew Linn, S. J. and Sheila Fabricant. *At Peace with the Unborn: A Book for Healing*. Mahwah, N.J.: Paulist Press, 1985.

Divorce

Allen, Charles L. *When a Marriage Ends*. Old Tappan, N.J.: Revell, 1986.

Mumford, Amy Ross. *When Divorce Ends Your Marriage It Hurts*. Denver: Accent Expressions, 1982.

Petri, Darlene. *The Hurt and Healing of Divorce*. Elgin, Ill.: David C. Cook, 1976.

———. *I Wish Someone Understood My Divorce*. Minneapolis: Augsburg, 1986.

Smoke, Jim. *Growing through Divorce*. Irvine, Calif.: Harvest House, 1976.

Stearns, Ann Kaiser. *Living through Personal Crisis*. New York: Ballantine Books, 1984.

Suicide

Baker, Don, and Emery Nester. *Finding Hope and Meaning in Life's Darkest Shadow*. Portland, Ore.: Multnomah, 1983.

Bloom, Lois A. *Mourning, after Suicide*. New York: Pilgrim Press, 1986.

Hewett, John H. *After Suicide*. Philadelphia: Westminster Press, 1980.

Stone, H. W. *Suicide and Grief*. Philadelphia: Fortess Press, 1972.

Support Groups for the Bereaved

American Association of Suicidology
Central Office
2459 South Ash
Denver, CO 80222
303-692-0985

The Candlelighters
Childhood Cancer Foundation
2025 Eye St., N.W., Suite 1011
Washington, D.C. 20006
202-659-5136

The Compassionate Friends
Therese Goodrich, Executive Director
P.O. Box 3696
Oak Brook, IL 60522-3696
312-990-0010

L.O.S.S.
(Loving Outreach for Survivors of Sudden Death)
13308-91 Street
Edmonton, Alberta
Canada T5E 3P8
403-476-7035

National Hospice Organization
1901 North Fort Meyer Drive
Suite 402
Arlington, VA 22209
703-243-5900

National Sudden Infant Death Syndrome Foundation
8200 Professional Place, Suite 104
Landover, MD 20785
301-459-3388

Parents Without Partners
8807 Coleseville Rd.
Silver Spring, MD 20910
301-588-9354

The Pregnancy and Infant Loss Center of Minnesota
1415 East Wayzata Blvd., Suite 22
Wayzata, MN 55391
612-473-9372

Widowed Persons Service
American Association of Retired Persons
1909 K. St., N.W.
Washington, D.C. 20049
202-728-4370

Best-selling author **H. Norman Wright** has written sixty-five books, including *Quiet Times for Couples, Making Peace with Your Past,* and *Tomorrow Can Be Different.* He is a marriage and family counselor, conducts grief-recovery seminars throughout the country, and is on the faculty at Talbot Graduate School of Theology. He and his wife, Joyce, live in Long Beach, California.

Griefshare is a video series for conducting grief-recovery support groups. The entire package offers thirteen videos that include interviews with thirty of the leading national experts in their field. It also contains students' and leaders' study guides. Phone 800-875-7560.